Orange Is the New Black
and Philosophy

Popular Culture and Philosophy® Series Editor: George A. Reisch

For full details of all Popular Culture and Philosophy® books, visit www.opencourtbooks.com.

Popular Culture and Philosophy®

Orange Is the New Black and Philosophy

Last Exit from Litchfield

EDITED BY

RICHARD GREENE AND
RACHEL ROBISON-GREENE

OPEN COURT
Chicago

Volume 92 in the series, Popular Culture and Philosophy ®, edited by George A. Reisch

**To find out more about Open Court books, call toll-free
1-800-815-2280, or visit our website at www.opencourtbooks.com**.

Open Court Publishing Company is a division of Carus Publishing Company,
dba Cricket Media.

Copyright © 2015 by Carus Publishing Company, dba Cricket Media

First printing 2015

ISBN: 978-0-8126-9899-2

Library of Congress Control Number: 2015943817

For Kristin Greene and Cheryl Hughes

Contents

Contents

Thanks

Working on this project has been a pleasure, in no small part because of the many fine folks who have assisted us along the way. In particular a debt of gratitude is owed to David Ramsay Steele and George Reisch at Open Court, Greta Gusteva Martela, the contributors to this volume, and our respective academic departments at UMass Amherst and Weber State University. Finally, we'd like to thank those family members, students, friends, and colleagues with whom we've had fruitful and rewarding conversations on various aspects of all things *Orange Is the New Black* as it relates to philosophical themes.

Learning from the Insiders

Welcome to cell block P ("P" is for Philosophy, of course). Your cell-block mates are an eclectic set of philosophers, who have been placed here for the things they have to say about philosophy and *Orange Is the New Black*.

Orange Is the New Black is both a book and a television series about the trials (both literally and figuratively), tribulations, and expoits of Piper (Kerman in the book, Chapman on the show). Piper is a middle class, white thirty-something woman who, while living what appears to be a fairly sheltered and very comfortable life, is arrested for her role in a drug smuggling ring, which she was involved with ten years earlier. The book and the show chronicle Piper's time in prison.

Orange Is the New Black is a wonderful show full of humor, drama, real life-situations, and a slew of characters from a host of backgrounds, who are forced to live together under the worst of all circumstances—incarceration. The writers and creators of the show do a fantastic job of exploring the various interrelations between the prisoners, between the members of the prison staff, between the prisoners and the prison staff,

and between the prisoners and their peeps on the outside (friends, family, lawyers, employers, accomplices,
etc.). The result is a book and a show that is ripe for
deep philosophical exploration. *Orange Is the New
Black* raises and in some cases resolves a number of
important philosophical issues, ranging from the role
of punishment in society to our moral obligations to our
fellow prisoners to existential themes to issues pertaining to race, gender, identity, and sexuality (just to name
a few).

Let us introduce you to some of your cell-mates.
Stephen Felder is here for his philosophical thoughts
on the topic of other minds. Myisha Cherry is doing
time for her thoughts on manipulation (it's prison; it
happens from time to time). Richard Greene is here because he has spent entirely too much of his life thinking about the Prisoner's Dilemma, including a
particular version of it raised by *Orange Is the New
Black*. Seth M. Walker explores religious themes in the
show (you may want to stay away from Pennsatucky).
Leigh Duffy, Christopher Hoyt, and Courtney Neal all
have different takes on existential themes in *Orange Is
the New Black*. (Seriously, does anything scream
"purely existential experience" more than doing hard
time?) Rod Carveth discusses *Orange* issues pertaining
to race. *Orange Is the New Black* is very much about
race and class relations. Chelsi Barnard Archibald sees
Crazy Eyes as a sort of modern-day Don Quixote.
Rachel Robison-Greene explores the moral obligations
of prisoners, contrasting them with our normal (read:
non-incarcerated) moral obligations. Christina DiEdoardo
explores transgender issues through a Nietzschean
perspective. Charlene Elsby and Rob Luzecky have
teamed up to take an Aristotelian look at friendship.
Christopher Ketcham looks at *Orange Is the New Black*

with the help of Jeremy Bentham's panopticon. And finally, what discussion of prison life would be complete without a treatment of Michel Foucault's views on the role of punishment? Jeff Stephenson and Sara Waller generously provide us with just such an account.

Now that you're here, you might as well sit back and take a look at what your cell-block mates have to say. You're not going anywhere for a while and you've got a lot of time on your hands. Enjoy the book!

I

Of course you are still going to have to go through initiation

1
Orange Is the New Black Can Change Your Life

CHRISTOPHER HOYT

There's a terrific exchange that takes place between Daya and Bennett late in Season Two that made me think about myself and how I had reacted to them in earlier episodes of *Orange Is the New Black*. Bennett and Daya are in a closet fooling around while they discuss their plan to frame Mendez:

> **BENNETT:** Okay, you know, I, I'm gonna tell Caputo that Mendez is the father.
>
> **DAYA:** But that's a lie.
>
> **BENNETT:** But didn't he have sex with you?
>
> **DAYA:** Yeah.
>
> **BENNETT:** Okay, so he's a criminal, he deserves to go to prison.
>
> **DAYA:** But you have sex with me. Used to, anyways.
>
> **BENNETT:** That's different. I, I love you.
>
> **DAYA:** So does he.

Could Daya really think that Mendez loves her? Mendez is a buffoon, a man too shallow and too phony to love anyone. To put the point another way, Mendez's character is written and performed to appear more like a cartoon than a man. Daya, on the other hand, comes across as a woman who is really learning to think for herself and to get in touch with her feelings.

Then suddenly it hit me that Bennett's love is only marginally more convincing than Mendez's. Bennett is certainly more capable of being authentic, so he's ahead of Pornstache on that score. But let's face it, aside from having sex, Bennett and Daya have done little more than flirt with each other like two grade school kids. Their courtship was literally characterized by passing secret notes and sharing gum. And yet, like a starry-eyed teenager, I had rooted for them in Season One. I found their flirtation endearing, and I contemplated the injustice of a system that kept apart two consenting adults hungry for intimacy.

Notes and gum? How could I have been such a sucker? I'm a grown man, for Pete's sake. Daya was out ahead of me here, doing the work that *Orange Is the New Black* does best: getting us to drop the little lies we tell ourselves and to see the world more honestly. Bennett and Daya have crushes on each other, and for all that crushes are fun and sometimes lead to love, they're not love. Their crush was never enough to overcome the impossible situation they were in, but by calling it "love," we all get to pretend that it is, somehow, justified, and that it might, somehow, work out.

While Daya's coming to see herself and the world more honestly, Bennett is still lost in self-serving lies. Not only does he call his crush on Daya "love," but he pretends that that love somehow absolves his crime, and he pretends that Mendez's crime justifies framing him. The fact of the matter is that what Bennett really wants is to get rid of Mendez, to hang on to Daya, and to avoid going to prison. The lines that he feeds himself are baloney, and Daya is now too far along in her own quest for authenticity to be fooled by them.

Pornstache, the Man

Let's go back to Pornstache for a minute, because his character can help us get a better handle on what's going on when we lie to ourselves. I said that Mendez is like a cartoon, and he is, but then a lot of real people also seem like cartoons. I'm thinking of those people who always seem to be performing a role, people who never at all seem relaxed and authentic. There are lots of people like that, really: the drama queens, the perpetually perky cheerleaders, the tireless braggarts. Ironically, I've got real doubts about some of the people who constantly advertise that they're "keeping it real." The thing is, you don't have to go too far down that hole before the distinction between what's real and what's an act ceases to make sense, even to yourself. The philosopher Jean-Paul Sartre says that such people are living in "bad faith," they have ceased to acknowledge, or even to know, how they really feel or what they really think (*Being and Nothingness*, p. 97). They're living in a state of extreme inauthenticity. Mendez seems to always be performing a part, the part of a blustering bully. His swagger and confidence are exaggerated, his intimidation of the prisoners a front to maintain control. It's as though he were an imperious prison guard playing the role of an imperious prison guard.

Pornstache is a relatively extreme case of someone living in bad faith, but we all do it sometimes, especially when the truth is inconvenient or unsavory. Bennett, Daya, Piper, Larry, Polly, Healy, and still more characters in *Orange Is the New Black* show signs of bad faith here and there. Quite a few story lines concern how those characters learn to be more authentic, and how they come to see the world more honestly for having done so. Daya, for example, only comes to see the foolishness of her flirtation with Bennett and the wrong of framing Mendez after months of thoughtlessly playing along, pursuing her selfish interests. Still more obviously, there's Piper, who arrives at Litchfield believing that she is an essentially good and innocent woman who doesn't belong amongst the "real" criminals she's locked up with. Within just a few episodes, that delusion melts into a far more complex understanding of crime, power, American society, and herself. Piper matures into a woman who knows who she really is and how the world really works.

Piper also reminds us that while dropping our acts of bad faith can sometimes be difficult, it feels good to get a more honest worldview. In "40 Oz. of Furlough," Piper is out of prison for a few days on a rare leave granted so that she can attend her grandmother's funeral—a ceremony that farcically morphs into her brother's wedding. Towards the end of the celebration, Piper sits with an elderly couple who seem to have known her since childhood. Having acknowledged Piper's situation, the woman reassuringly tells Piper that they still see her as the girl they always knew and admired, and the man says, "I'm sure you're anxious to return to your old self." Piper pensively responds, "I'm not, actually." Who would want to go back to self-deception and a distorted worldview after having seen the truth? Piper has dropped her shield of bad faith. She is more authentic, and her understanding of the world is, too. Moments later, in a convenience store, we watch

Piper choose a bottle of Colt 45 over a sparkling wine in a gesture reaffirming that she prefers her new self and her new vision of the world. Notice that Piper embraces her new perspective, not her life in prison or the life of an outlaw. Piper doesn't knock up the liquor store, she merely grabs a bottle and enjoys her few hours of freedom before voluntarily returning to prison. It's Piper's budding authenticity that defines the growth, the emerging depth, of her character.

You Just Can't Fake It

If you've ever been through a prolonged bad stretch of life, you might know how appealing it is to think that you can change your worldview at will. *Orange Is the New Black* is there to remind you that you can't. Think back to the scene when Healy goes to see a therapist, Chris Maser, apparently to talk about his explosive temper. Although he says only that he is there because "more than one person" suggested that he speak to someone, Healy almost immediately describes how his whole life is uncomfortable because of "all these women, these criminals, these bureaucratic idiots." He used to like his job, Healy continues, he used to feel useful.

MASER: And what changed?

HEALY: Hell if I know. I got older. Maybe I care less. Maybe I've seen enough to know that I won't make a difference. That it's all a waste.

MASER: You know, sometimes we get stuck seeing things from one perspective, but if we can just shift our perspective even a little bit, makes all the difference.

HEALY: That's it? That's your fancy, $75-an-hour advice?

Within moments, Healy is so frustrated with Maser's glib advice that he flies into a rage and curses at her. This is a new side of Healy, or at least a new extreme, and it's tempting to condemn him for his foul disposition and his lack of self-control. Yet at the same time, Healy's frustration with Maser is understandable even if his response is indecent. Her guidance is just too shallow to be helpful. You can't change your outlook on life at will. A pessimist might like to be an optimist, an atheist might wish that she believed in God, and a gourmet might want to delight in cheese doodles, but none of them can change how they see and experience the world simply because it would be convenient or pleasing. Neither can Healy see the prison system or himself as he once did just because that would make him feel better, or even because he has the nagging intuition that his outlook is too cynical.

It's tempting to think that a change of outlook is really just a change of mood, as though Healy only needs to cheer up and be pleasant. After all, you might say, you can't change the world, but you can change your attitude. The problem is that if you try to force a change of mood without a change in your perception of reality, you can only keep up the fakery for so long. That's just the point of "Take a Break from Your Values," in which we watch both Healy and Sister Ingalls crash down to Earth from the phony worlds they try to live in.

Sister Ingalls has managed to feign indifference to Soso's hunger strike only through a great effort of will, but her real desire to martyr herself for social change finally gets the better of her. In a parallel story, Healy forces a manner of calm and caring with the prisoners despite his real feelings and beliefs, even when he is dealing with the maddening Pennsatucky. He asks Piper to contribute to his corny "Feeling Jar" despite her obvious unease with it, and he organizes Safe Place, a support group in which prisoners are encouraged to feel comfortable and to share their feelings openly despite the glaring realities of prison life. "What happens in Safe Place stays in Safe Place," Healy absurdly tells the women. To make sure that we get the point, at the one and only meeting of Safe Place that anyone attends, Healy asks Poussey to open up and talk about how she got hurt even while Poussey's attacker, Suzanne, looks on menacingly. Safe Place is a fantasy where Healy lives at a distance from reality, a lot like how Mendez lives in bubble of cartoonish performance.

Healy's ill-conceived Safe Place fails, of course, but his stilted efforts have created a bond between him and Pennsatucky that just might change his perspective after all. When Healy and Pennsatucky collude privately regarding how he might reach out to her fellow inmates, at first sight he seems to be using her only to get to the others. But in fact he treats Pennsatucky as a person worthy of collusion, of inclusion, at a time when the other prisoners have shut her out. For Pennsatucky, this is a profound and moving experience, and in the final episode of Season Two, "We Have Manners, We're Polite," she tries to tell Healy so. She confronts him in the rec room, and, sensing that he is characteristically angry and distant, she maneuvers to break through to him, to get him to really see the depth of her feelings. "I am forever grateful to you," Pennsatucky tells Healy, "'Cause you're the only person in my whole life that's ever taken the time to talk to me. And it just seems like you're really good at what you do and that you really care." While Healy was looking right through Pennsatucky in hopes of forming a meaningful connection with the other prisoners, the thing he wanted was right under his nose, just waiting to be seen. Here it is, Pennsatucky is signaling to Healy, the aspect of the world that you want to see is right here! The episode and the season end without clear evidence that Healy has grasped the significance of what passed between him and Pennsatucky, but the look on his face and his efforts to save Suzanne from wrongful conviction suggest that he has come to see the humanity and the vulnerability of the inmates once again.

Healy's encounter with Pennsatucky reminds us that the experiences that change our worldview usually come unbidden and affect us in ways we could not have anticipated. Healy can no more will himself to believe that he can do real good at Litchfield than he can will himself to believe that he he's a dead ringer for Brad Pitt. People who try to will or command a change of worldview often get something very different than what they expected. Think of what happens to people who, in search of change, go on missions, volunteer for war, or have babies. Many a missionary has lost his own faith instead of inspiring it in others, war has ruined the spirits and minds of countless soldiers who went eagerly in search of adventure, and parenthood seems to surprise just about everyone who tries it. Healy might come to see the world anew, but his phony efforts with Safe Place aren't going to get him there.

How to Love a Crazy Fuckin' Hillbilly

The dawning and dimming of aspects has everything to do with our ethical sense. In Season One, Piper displays her moral sensitivity by remaining attuned to the humanity in Pennsatucky, despite that Piper can also see that Pennsatucky is a dimwitted, dangerous, "crazy fuckin' hillbilly." Piper sees that, but she also sees that Pennsatucky is a woman capable of suffering, and she sees the moral significance of that suffering. When the plan that Alex hatched to get Pennsatucky locked away in the psychiatric ward works, Piper feels pity and remorse. Alex, by contrast, only sees Pennsatucky as a problem. When Piper suggests going to the authorities with the truth that will get Pennsatucky released from Psych, Alex responds, "Look, you're just hung over and feeling emo, all right? She's exactly where she belongs. We basically performed a public service." But Piper can't let it go, and she does arrange Pennsatucky's release.

On the other hand, in Season Two, Piper is blind to Soso's humanity, and, at least for a moment, appears as cold and morally bankrupt as Alex. I'm thinking of the episode in which Piper, in an effort to get back a blanket (!), tries to trick Soso into being Boo's prison wife. Even when Soso realizes what's going on and confronts her, Piper appears mostly unfazed:

Soso: You tried to sell me for a blanket?

Piper: Well, when you put it that way . . .

Soso: You are sick, you know that? You are seriously fucked up.

Boo: You know, she's right, Chapman. You're a horrible person.

Soso and Boo are right about Piper, at least in that moment, Piper has behaved atrociously. Piper's blindness to Soso's humanity has everything to do with the particular stresses of prison, where the women seem to constantly bargain and scheme and double-cross for the most basic of comforts. The point of the scene is to show that Piper is becoming one of them, a woman as morally bankrupt as her context. The scene is striking because it shows how much Piper has changed. But just what has changed? Has she truly gone blind to Soso's humanity? I think it's far more realistic to think that she has suppressed her awareness out of convenience. It's as though Piper were playing the part of a hardened criminal because it serves her interests to do so. She's living in bad faith, still capable of seeing the wretchedness of her conduct, but choosing not to for the selfish reasons.

Ludwig Wittgenstein is widely regarded as the first or second most important philosopher of the twentieth century, and one of the ten or twenty most important philosophers of all time. Wittgenstein had many great insights, but the one that is especially useful to our discussion of *Orange Is the New Black* is that to perceive the meaning of something—a word, a gesture, a television show—is to perceive an aspect of it (*Philosophical Investigations*, p. 214). You can start to get Wittgenstein's point if you think about the different aspects of human gestures. Think about the opening scene of the first episode of *Orange Is the New Black,* when Taystee watches Piper shower and compliments her on her "perky tits." An aspect-blind Piper might simply miss that Taystee is trying to intimidate her, that Taystee is deliberately violating her privacy. The meaning of the "compliment" is not to compliment, and it takes a sensitivity to the nuance of human gesture to pick up on its real significance. You'd have to be pretty slow to miss that aspect of Taystee's gesture—to think simply, hey, she sure is being nice—but you don't have to be especially slow to miss many other meanings all around you. We do it all the time, and *Orange Is the New Black* has something to teach us about the experience of what it's like to lose sight of them, and, what it's like to gain sight of them.

What Just Happened to Me?

Orange Is the New Black presents us again and again with characters who, due to their own callowness and selfishness, are blind to significant aspects of the word, characters who seem to miss ethically significant dimensions that they ought to see. Take the love affair between Larry and Polly. While we can understand their attraction to each other, and possibly even their choice to have sex, their claim to be in love is clearly portrayed as premature and forced. Recall the scene in which the two visit Piper in prison to confess their love.

They sit awkwardly holding hands and using expressions like "We have decided" as they act out the part of a long-established couple. Polly opens the conversation by saying to Piper, absurdly, "Please tell us you don't hate us, because you're still my best friend." To say that to Piper in that moment marks Polly as being almost as disconnected from reality as Morello (the inmate who lives in a perpetual fantasy that she will one day marry that man she is jailed for having stalked). The same goes for Polly's final defense, the one that sounds like the final defense of so many selfish and short-sighted love affairs: "But we didn't decide to love each other, Piper, it just happened. The way love does." Here is that tired, old dodge: I'm not responsible for my actions or their moral consequences, love made me do it.

Piper, having evolved into a woman of integrity, responds with truth. Piper says to Larry, "The first person that you fuck after we break up is my best friend. My married best friend." Her slow, angry delivery gives us time to think about Larry's choice. No matter what he might tell himself, Larry simply is the sort of man who has cuckolded a friend, deeply hurt his imprisoned ex, and ruined the relationship of two close friends. Larry's claim to love Polly can't absolve him of his depravity any more than Bennett's claim to love Daya absolves him of his crime. "And then you did the worst thing," Piper continues, now addressing Larry and Polly both, "You decided to fall in love." Polly and Larry are acting in bad faith, and Piper calls them out on it. They have indulged themselves in the dreamy fantasy that love is an unstoppable force of good, and they repeat that lie to themselves in an attempt to evade responsibility for their actions. Larry's stilted use of "we" and Polly's doe-eyed tale of being blind-sided by love are expressions of bad faith, they are flights from the reality of who they are and what they've done.

Poor Larry appears destined to live in his cocoon of bad faith forever, trapped in a worldview distorted by self-serving aspect-blindness. Unlike Piper, there are no clear signs that he's learning to be more authentic. However, the sacrifice of his character is for the benefit of at least some of us who are watching. Mind you, I don't mean those self-righteous viewers who delight in yuppie-bashing, an indulgence that the show encourages too much of. No, I mean that a lot of us in the audience identify with Larry in ways that might help us grow by seeing him fail. Consider Larry's distasteful part in "Fucksgiving." Larry has just published an essay about his experience of being engaged to a convict in the *New York Times* weekly column, "Modern Love." The title of the essay lets us know that his essay is vulgarly self-indulgent: "One Sentence, Two Prisoners." At Thanksgiving dinner, Larry fortuitously sits next to a nerdy reporter in geeky-hipsters glasses named Maury Kind who hosts an NPR show that apparently features people telling stories about their own lives. Maury has read Larry's essay, and Larry grovels in hopes of having his story aired. Kind derisively let's Larry know how he really sees him. "Well, I thought your column was an interesting perspective," Kind says sarcastically, "You know, the long-suffering husband." "Fiancé," Larry responds sheepishly, "I mean, I didn't really mean for it to come off that way." Intend it or not, Larry's essay *did* come off that way, and he looks like a shallow jerk.

Have you enjoyed "Modern Love" on a Sunday morning? I have. Did you spot that Maury Kind is modeled after Ira Glass, host of NPR's *This American Life*? I did. I'm part of the target audience, it seems, and also the target of an implicit critique. I like "Modern Love," but it does tend to focus on the problems of the privileged, problems that must sound as trite and self-indulgent to the truly troubled as Larry's essay sounds to the women in Litchfield. Just imagine how Rosa (the bank robber dying of cancer) might react to the "Modern Love" essay of December 15th 2013, in which a woman tells the story of how her marriage got a boost when her cynical husband let down his guard during a yoga retreat in Costa Rica. The new Piper, the Piper who guzzles Colt 45, has more on her mind, and *Orange Is the New Black* reminds me that I should, too.

Orange Is the New Black has a way of breaking through the fourth wall like that, a way of working on *me* and not only on the characters. It's affecting my worldview. As Wittgenstein says, changes of aspect come in many varieties (*Last Writings on the Philosophy of Psychology*, §694). It's one thing to notice that Taylor Schilling looks kind of like Katy Perry, and quite another to notice that Litchfield looks a lot like high school. It's one thing for viewers to try to accept Piper and Larry's magnificent brownstone as a plausible home for two marginally employed New Yorkers, and quite another for Marcus to try to accept Sophia (the transgender hairdresser) as his father.

Orange Is the New Black excels at inducing the sort of aspect shifts that come when we get in touch with ourselves more fully, when we acknowledge those lingering doubts and vague intuitions that haunt our cozy worldviews. I knew that Bennett and Daya were being silly and foolish from the start, but I allowed myself to vicariously enjoy the pleasures of their crush and many of the lies that they told themselves in order to indulge it. Healy probably has a notion that his dark view of the prisoners at Litchfield has everything to do with his rotten marriage and his loneliness. With luck, Pennsatucky's unexpected friendship and gratitude might restore his capacity to see the humanity of the inmates. I haven't got much hope for Pornstache, but were he to look inside himself, I expect that he would realize that what he calls a love for Daya is really the thrill of finally allowing a spot of human tenderness to pass through that armature of machismo and cruelty. His dramatic exit in handcuffs plays as comedy, but we can also see it as the tragic last performance of a man whose worldview is wildly distorted by bad faith.

And you, Dear Reader, has watching *Orange Is the New Black* helped you to develop a more authentic worldview?

2
Should We Give a Ship?

RACHEL ROBISON-GREENE

When we get invested in television shows, we frequently root for certain characters to get together. There are whole blogs and universes of fan fiction dedicated to exploring what it would be like if certain beloved characters got together—notably Olivia Bensen and Elliott Stabler from *Law and Order SVU*, Mulder and Scully from *The X-Files,* or Hermione and Ron from the Harry Potter movies—spoiler alert, that one worked out!

The kids call it "shipping." Here's what the Urban Dictionary has to say about it: ship "(v) To endorse a romantic relationship." Fan fiction aficionados take it a little further. Here, again, from the Urban Dictionary, a definition of "shipping": "A term used to describe fan fictions that take previously created characters and put them as a pair. It usually refers to romantic relationships, but it can refer to platonic ones as well. (Just think of "shipping" as short for "relationship".)" For the rest of our discussion here, I'm going to drop the scare quotes around the word "ship" and just treat it as a regular word. I'm a millennial, after all.

Though most of us probably aren't spending our free time writing fan fiction about it (not that there's anything wrong with that), if you're in possession of this book, there are probably *Orange Is the New Black* characters that you'd like to see end up together (Piper and Alex? Taystee and Poussey?) The thing with shipping, though, is that it does not seem to be subject to many of the standards that we bring to bear when we evaluate the relationships of the people to whom we are close in real life. Why should it? We're dealing with fictional characters (most of the time) after all. Are there any real standards that we employ when we ship characters from television shows?

Standard Shipping

In the real world, our loved ones frequently enter into relationships that make us facepalm (or worse). If we're brave enough, we might try to talk to them about their poor choices. We might try to get them to see their partner's character flaws or to anticipate the potential future hardships that might come with staying with a particular person.

Our best friend's partner might have a troubling lack of ambition or work ethic, our sister's partner might be abusive, or our co-worker might be dating someone who has just never fully emotionally matured into a functioning adult. Outside of the television universe, we want people, especially those that we care about, to act in a way that's consistent with their long-term self-interest.

What are we doing when we ship TV characters? Is there any rhyme or reason to it? Are there good ships and bad ships? Can one viewer ship better than another viewer? Are we thinking about these matters in any sort of principled way? Our attitudes about the romantic lives of characters don't seem arbitrary. Something guides our opinions. What is it? What should it be?

Most of the time, we don't ship for ethical reasons— because we think it would be morally good for two characters to get together. Mostly, we ship for aesthetic reasons—

because it would be cool for them to get together. Ethics comes into it occasionally, but usually we ship a certain brace of characters because we think, artistically, that it would be fun, or beautiful, or otherwise satisfying.

Shipping Whom We Shouldn't

There may be weirdos out there who are rooting for Voldemort and Molly Weasley to get together. There is the *Saturday Night Live* mock trailer where Ultron pairs up with Black Widow. Perhaps there are small groups of *Orange Is the New Black* fans who want Vee and Soso to establish a love connection, but that isn't usually how it goes.

We usually end up wanting the characters to get together in a way that's consistent with the intent of the creators of the show. So, for example, there are some live relationship possibilities that are obvious in *Orange Is the New Black*. Like me, you might root for Alex and Piper. If you're some sort of yuppie, you might want Piper to end up with Larry instead. You might want to see Taystee and Poussey end up together, or even, just for laughs, Pennsatucky and Big Boo.

It's pretty clear, though, that when we root for certain characters to get together on television shows, we do not often have the long-term self-interests of the characters at heart. If you're a *Buffy the Vampire Slayer* fan, did you ever really want Buffy to end up with Riley? He was the stable, earnest, boy scout love interest that you might only barely remember from Season Four. I'm guessing you didn't really ship the two of them. You probably shipped Buffy and Angel or Buffy and Spike. In truth, though, both Spike and Angel would have been *horrible* for Buffy in, so to speak, real life.

The same is true on *Orange Is the New Black*. Piper's the main character, so, presumably we're supposed to care about her romantic life. Despite Piper's own flaws, the show is pretty successful in getting us to do that. The advice we'd likely feel inclined to give Piper based on our interests in the plot of the show is not likely to be the advice we would give to someone we cared about.

Let's, for a moment, apply the standards that we would ordinarily apply to our friends or family to Piper and the relationships that she chooses. Many philosophers, including heavyweights like Plato and Aristotle, think that true friendship is intimately connected to virtue and human flourishing. If the flourishing of both parties is a primary goal of the relationship, there are some common-sense standards that need to be met. Here are some ideas that come immediately to mind:

1. Long-term safety and security. Many elements of relationships fall under this general umbrella. Most obviously, for a person to be safe in the long term, their relationship partner can't be physically abusive. They can't be willing to routinely put their partner in harm's way. Long term safety and security might also involve a certain financial component. I'm not saying here that you should hook up with someone for their money, but you don't want a partner that threatens the roof over your head or the basic safety of your living conditions.

2. Capacity to satisfy emotional needs. Good relationship partners are empathetic. They try to understand what it is like to be in their partner's shoes and they adjust their behavior appropriately when they judge that it makes sense to do so.

3. Trust. It's important that we feel comfortable telling our partners things that we don't want them to share with others. We need to feel safe giving advice to and taking advice from them.

4. The willingness to let one another grow. It isn't healthy for people to remain static. It is important for us all to continue to set goals for ourselves and to try to achieve those goals. This is part of how we lead meaningful, satisfying lives. Continuing to improve our characters is also what helps us to become virtuous individuals, so it is important to be with someone who makes this growth possible and perhaps even to be with someone who encourages it.

Let's see how our favorite *Orange Is the New Black* "ships" hold up to these basic standards. Let's start with the relationship I love to ship—Alex and Piper. The backstory alone makes it quite clear that Alex does not provide Piper with long-term safety and security. She also does not enable or encourage Piper to find safety and security for herself. Instead, she enables the type of behavior that results in Piper engaging in criminal activity and ending up in jail. Alex doesn't fare so well here.

How does Larry do? Piper gives up her adventurous, dangerous lifestyle with Alex and goes on to pursue a much calmer, more normal looking existence with Larry. Larry is pursuing a career in writing (or, perhaps a more accurate way to put it is that he is just waiting for a writing career to fall into his lap). Piper and her friend Polly start up a business that sells designer homemade soaps. There may be problems with a life lived in this way, especially when the person living it has a personality like Piper's, but if we are judging this relationship purely on the basis of its tendency to promote safety and security, this one looks pretty promising.

When it comes to long-term safety and security then, I'd say the win would have to go to Larry. He's not a drug dealer like Alex, so that one is really no big surprise.

What about the capacity to satisfy Piper's emotional needs? It's not clear that either Alex or Larry does this particularly well. There are times when Alex seems to really get Piper. They often appear to have a closer relationship than the one Piper and Larry share. Some of the main story arcs with Larry involve a lack of ability on his part to really fully try to understand what it must be like for Piper to survive in prison.

Early on, it often seems as if Larry is just waiting for Piper to get out so that they can resume the life that they had before, not realizing that prison is likely to be an experience that would profoundly change Piper. One of the most revealing plot developments on this point takes place when Larry writes the story for the paper on what it's like to have a fiancée who's in prison. The article focuses on Larry's experience, but when it comes to the description of Piper's world, the article falls flat. Larry is unable to really capture what things are like for Piper, not because of a lack of writing skill, but because Larry does not do his best to empathize with her, to actually understand how she might have been transformed by her prison experience.

Even so, in the moments when Piper and Alex seem to be really clicking, the viewer can just never be sure if anyone is telling the truth. The two seem to have a genuine affection for one another. Alex seems to be able to see a wild, adventurous part of Piper about which Larry is oblivious. All the same, I can't feel good about giving this one to Alex either because of her manipulative nature. Both Larry and Alex sort of suck when it comes to satisfying the emotional needs of others. This is perhaps because we are dealing with a group of narcissists. Let's call this one a draw.

It does not require a sustained period of viewing of *Orange Is the New Black* to realize that trust is sort of an issue on the show with all of the characters. There is no one that anyone can really trust. Not the other prisoners, not the guards; even the people on the outside like Larry and Polly lie and cheat and violate one another's trust when it suits them. Alex is untrustworthy from the start. She sells Piper out in order to get a better deal for herself at the beginning of the series. That's what lands Piper in jail in the first place. Later, in Season Two, when Piper has the opportunity to testify against a hard-core drug dealer in order to get an early release, Alex convinces Piper not to do it. Alex tells Piper that they will both be in danger if the drug dealer is not convicted. Following Alex's orders, Piper gets on the stand and lies. Alex does not follow her own advice. She gets on the stand and tells the truth about the drug dealer and obtains early release. Piper is stuck in jail, looking at increased jail time for perjury.

Of course, Piper isn't too trustworthy herself. She cheated on Larry in prison with Alex. Larry doesn't seem too keen to avoid betrayal either, though. He and Polly have an affair while Polly is still married. On this score, again, nobody wins. No one is really deserving of trust.

The healthiest relationships are conducted in such a way that it makes it possible for both partners to learn and to grow. This is that crucial element of friendship that the ancient Greek philosophers spent so much time talking about. Larry, for one, seems to have a very narrow conception of Piper's growth—one that allows her to grow only along the yuppie dimension of development that he imagined her progressing toward when he met her.

It's not clear that Alex has much of a picture, either for herself or for anyone else, of what a flourishing life would look like. It isn't clear that anyone is going to do any growing in a relationship with her.

The lesson may be—at the end of the day, that perhaps we really shouldn't be shipping any of these people! If any of our friends or family wanted to date almost any of the characters from *Orange Is the New Black*, we'd advise them to run from the situation as fast as they can. We're all flawed though, so relationships can only be so good, even off screen.

At least in my case, I don't think it's the hope for the flourishing virtue of my favorite characters that makes me ship them with anyone. Flawed characters are often the best ones. In truth, I probably don't ship Piper and Larry because Larry is sort of an uninteresting dweeb. It is likely that I do ship Piper and Alex because Laura Prepon is attractive, has a deep, sultry voice, and the character seems smart and a little devious. The same might be true of many of my other ships as well. I mean, consider Mulder and Scully from *The X-Files*. Those characters are written in to have perceptions of the world that are dramatically differently from one another. Mulder is so charming and Scully so sensible that we root for them, even though their relationship in real life wouldn't have a snowball's chance in hell of working out. This is probably true more often than not with the characters that I ship.

Ship It Back

Even if our ordinary, run-of-the-mill shippings don't turn out to be routinely motivated by the flourishing of fictional characters, I do think that there might be some basic moral rules to follow when it comes to shipping. That may be entirely wrong. It may be that relationships in art don't need to be governed by any rules at all. On the other hand, popular media does often set the standard for how we should feel about certain behavior, so we might want to have some basic principles in mind. If there are any rules, here are a few thoughts for what some of them might be:

1. Don't ship Pornstache with anyone. I'm clearly sort of joking here, but look at the kind of guy Pornstache is. He's the kind of guy who coerces people into engaging in sexual acts by withholding from them basic privileges. He's the kind of guy who will lock someone in a closet, knowing they are having a serious problem, until they die of a drug overdose. Alex and Larry may not be ideal relationship partners, but Pornstache deserves to be in prison as much or more than anyone on the show. Our hearts may soften when Pornstasche seems to be in love with Daya, knowing as we do that Daya sexually manipulated Pornstasche to explain the possibility of her pregnancy.

Everyone is human and is subject to the potential for manipulation. If our moral attitudes toward characters are bound by any rules at all, though, forgiving a person who is essentially a serial rapist and hoping they hook up with someone nice is, perhaps, a restriction we should put in place when it comes to taking on attitudes toward characters. This isn't a call for any form of censorship, but, rather, a suggestion about how we personally engage television shows.

2. Don't ship people who aren't capable of giving consent. Don't ship relationships between adults and children. This one gets to be kind of muddy, since many of the most complicated relationships occur with partners between which there is an imbalance of power. The issue of consent is a contentious one, philosophically.

3. Don't ship or not ship on the basis of a character's race, gender, sexual orientation, or gender identity. What I mean by this is, don't refrain from shipping Piper and Crazy Eyes simply because they are not the same race. You can refrain from shipping them because of the fact that Crazy Eyes urinated openly in Piper's prison cell, but don't put restrictions in place on the basis of race.

Similarly, don't rule relationships out because you don't want homosexual characters to exist (if you are a person like that, you're watching the wrong show!). The same goes with wanting someone to be lonely because you don't approve of their gender identity.

None of these constraints are constraints regarding what the actual content of a television show should be. One of the great things about television, like other art, is that it transports us inside of these little hypothetical scenarios. We can explore what we might do, or what we think it would be appropriate for other people to do, in scenarios that are utterly foreign to our everyday lives. These scenarios provide us with little ethical, philosophical thought experiments. All sorts of things that would be devastating, horrible events in the real world (consider *The Walking Dead* here), make for great television. The range of possible responses is wide. Some of these responses are shipping responses. Though we may ship mainly on the basis of aesthetic concerns, they also provide opportunities to test our moral intuitions about relationships and behavior in general.

All of that said, one of the couples I have historically shipped the hardest is Clarice Starling and Hannibal Lecter, so take my comments with the weight you now think that they deserve.

II

How's this whole 'agenda' thing work?

3
Nietzsche and a Trans Woman Walk into a Prison

CHRISTINA A. DIEDOARDO, ESQ.

I have a shameful secret. Until relatively recently, I was the only trans woman on the planet (or so it seemed) who hadn't watched *Orange Is the New Black*, and who wasn't completely gaga over Laverne Cox's portrayal of Sophia Burset, the only trans woman incarcerated at the Litchfield Federal Correctional Institute.

Some of my reluctance to give the show a chance stemmed from what I do for a living. After transitioning in 2005 in law school and passing the bar, I've worked as a criminal defense attorney. Few things are more professionally and personally difficult than watching a trans client get sentenced to custody, because I know far too well what's likely in store for them.

Most of the trans clients I've represented have been male-to-female transsexuals and have been pre-operative, meaning they (like many, if not most) trans women haven't undergone the genital reassignment surgery (GRS) supposedly necessary to make us "women" in the eyes of jail and prison administrators. As a result, *most* trans women get incarcerated in male prisons, where they're at a severely elevated risk for harassment, assault, rape, and worse.

In that context, Burset is an outlier, because she's post-operative when she gets to Litchfield. However, the rest of her backstory is familiar to me and many others. She's doing time because she financed that surgery (which, in the real world, *still* isn't covered by insurance in most states and can run to five figures) by a series of credit-card frauds. Whether intended or not, Burset's crime is a nice shout-out to the real-life Dee Farmer, the trans woman (and master forger) who, after being raped in a male facility, fought her resulting civil case against the prison all the way to the US Supreme Court and then went on to secure a compassionate release and fake her own death (which everyone believed until she was arrested later on a new charge).

Orange annoyed me at first because I felt like Dee Farmer (indeed, almost all of my real-life trans clients) would run rings around Burset if they were in the same facility. In the interest of being completely honest to you the reader, some of me also thought "If we're going to have trans criminals on television, can't they at least be effective and intimidating criminals?"

However, after watching through the end of Season Two, I came to a new appreciation of Burset's character. Like most things in this life, it's Friedrich Nietzsche's fault.

A Philosopher and a Trans Woman Go to Prison

I analyze philosophy through my filters as a lawyer and an activist, so two of Nietzsche's ideas have stuck with me. The first is "What does not destroy me, makes me stronger" from *Twilight of the Idols* and the second is the concept of the *"Übermensch"*, or super human, from his works *The Gay Science* and *Thus Spoke*

Zarathustra. With slight modifications, both are apt descriptions of Burset's character.

First, let's look at Burset's criminal charges. She's in prison on a federal credit-card fraud beef and—given what we see of her in "Lesbian Request Denied"—potentially an identity theft count (from her rifling through the files of fire victims while working as a firefighter). Under 15 U.S.C. 1644, anyone who "knowingly in a transaction affecting interstate or foreign commerce, uses or attempts or conspires to use any counterfeit, fictitious, altered, forged, lost, stolen, or fraudulently obtained credit card" in a transaction or transactions worth an aggregate of $1,000 in a one-year period is subject to a federal sentence of either a fine of up to $10,000 *or* a sentence of up to ten years in prison.

That means a judge could theoretically sentence her to a fine only, probation, or any random custodial sentence up to a decade. In reality, although the Sentencing Guidelines have not been mandatory for almost a decade, they still are *seen* as virtually mandatory by most federal judges, which cuts down their discretion.

The Guidelines work as a matrix where the offense level of the crime is on the *y*-axis; while the defendant's criminal history (in category I–VI, in increasing order of severity) is on the *x*-axis. The point where the axes intersect lists a guideline range of months in custody.

While we lack a lot of the information needed to completely evaluate where Burset would fall, we can make some assumptions. She was a firefighter, so it's likely her prior criminal history was non-existent and she'd be in Category I. Under the Guidelines, the base offense level for credit card fraud with no priors is six. Assuming less than $120,000 of losses (in contrast to say, Piper Chapman, who committed her money drug mule crimes either out of love or *ennui*, Burset had a specific goal she was working towards) bumps the offense level by eight, to 13. We don't know (yet, anyway) how many people she victimized, but let's say it was at least fifty people but less than 250, which increases the offense level to 17.

That gives us a Guideline sentence of 24–30 months on what is arguably the most victimless crime of any prisoner in Litchfield. Credit card customers are never personally liable for frauds committed on their account and credit card companies can mitigate much, if not all, of their risk of garden-variety fraud and loss either via insurance or by writing off the losses at tax time.

By comparison, Chapman is doing fifteen months for participating in an international heroin conspiracy where she helped move hundreds of thousands of dollars across international borders while working closely with organized crime figures in the US and elsewhere distributing an addictive substance that kills people.

Some might argue this evident sentencing disparity has nothing to do with the fact that Burset is a working class trans woman of color and Chapman is an upper-class, bright-faced white cisgender (the term means a person whose identity is congruent with the gender they were assigned at birth) woman. However, I will not insult your intelligence by attempting to do so.

The Why of Life

Besides being sentenced to more time than her crimes would appear to deserve, Burset faces a set of unique indignities from the prison staff, her family, *and* her fellow prisoners that she must endure to rise above.

In Season One's "Lesbian Request Denied," the prison decides to mess with Burset's hormone dosage (which, by the way, is a violation of the Eighth Amendment's ban on cruel and unusual punishment by denying prisoners access to necessary medical care) apparently for the hell of it. She's repeatedly misgendered and mocked by prison staff—witness Assistant Warden Natalie Figueroa's quip "Why would anyone want to give up being a man? It's like winning the lottery and giving the ticket back"—and has to take radical DIY measures just to *see* a medical professional.

Meanwhile, we see flashbacks of her life before Litchfield with Burset's spouse, Crystal. While Crystal was supportive of Burset's transition on some superficial levels—such as helping her with clothes—there's a major limit to that support, as we soon discover.

"I'm fine with the rest of it," Crystal tells Burset. "The hair and the makeup, I'll teach you all of it. You'll be a pro. *Just please keep your penis*" (emphasis added).

In other words, Crystal's support is conditional on Burset's granting her exclusive authority over the most intimate decision a trans woman can make—whether or not Burset should undergo gender reassignment surgery. To Burset's credit, she explicitly tells Crystal that's not a decision she can cede to her, which sets up Crystal's revenge when she visits Burset after the prison decides to mess with her hormone therapy.

Burset asks Crystal to smuggle in hormones from the outside, which she refuses to do (as is her right of course). But things escalate quickly from there. "I married a man named Marcus," says Crystal. "I cry for him all the time." Then she drops the H-bomb: "You wanna make it up to me? Do your time. *Get the fuck out of here, so you can be a father to your son. Man up*" (emphasis added).

It's hard for me to watch that episode or read that previous sentence without feeling the knife in my own gut, as if those words were being said to me. One of the things non-trans folks figure out quickly is that refusing to recognize our gender identity, no matter where we are in the process, is one of the most efficient ways to torture us. Effectively, it negates our personhood and is another way of saying "Humans get to define themselves. You're not even human. I, an outside observer, have the power to decide whether you're a man or a woman regardless of your feelings in the matter according to my biases, prejudices, and half-truths and you have no say in this discussion."

Her bunkies at Litchfield follow a similar script. Although she provides an important service to her colleagues by working in the hair salon, in "Lesbian Request Denied" she's repaid with insults like these. "I wouldn't let that he-she touch my hair with a ten-foot pole." When Burset seeks help from Galina "Red" Reznikov to use her smuggling network (which brings in non-narcotic contraband like pantyhose) to help her get hormones, Red bellows "You, I don't understand you. *I got three sons, and let me tell you, if they tried to do what you did, I'd chop off their hands before I'd let them get rid of their baby makers*" (emphasis added).

Not only is Burset at the center of a perfect triangular storm of abuse from the prison administration, her family, and her fellow prisoners, she must effectively face that storm alone. Even a whiny, over-privileged rich kid like Chapman can access support from Nicky Nichols, from Chapman's ex-girlfriend Alex Vause (though that support often comes with consequences), or from Lorna Morello. *Burset has nobody*. She doesn't fit with Yvonne "Vee" Parker's gang of African-American prisoners any more than she fits in with "Red's Girls" or the various ad hoc coalitions that Chapman seems destined to form and dissipate with the consistency of a tropical storm.

But Burset triumphs, somehow, because all of these threats and indignities—as dangerous as they are—aren't enough individually or in the aggregate to end her life by their own powers or persuade her to take that step. As Nietzsche points out in *Twilight of the Idols* "If we possess our *why* of life we can put up with almost any *how*. Man does not strive after happiness; only the Englishman does that."

Burset is assuredly no Englishwoman. Her *why* of life is bringing her body into conformity with her gender identity. The *how*—whether it's the credit card frauds she committed to pay for her surgeries or the things that happen to her in Litchfield as a consequence of that decision—are of secondary importance.

Ironically and without realizing it, Burset's prisoner colleagues act on Nietzsche's advice in other areas as well. Burset is patient, calm and eschews violence as a means to pursue her goals. From a macro level, this makes her one of the most courageous prisoners in Litchfield. It also explains why she's shunned. "If a woman possesses manly virtues one should run away from her," writes Nietzsche "and if she does not possess them she runs away herself."

Indeed, it's only when Burset learns to embrace her dual status as a trans woman and a female prisoner that she's able to migrate from being seen as a sub-human freak to a person with unique knowledge to offer.

From Unterfrau to Übertrans

In Season One's "WAC Pack," despite not being a member of the African-American clique, Burset runs for the Women's Advisory Council and tries to take the high road, telling her colleagues "My friends, we may be incarcerated, but that does not mean we're not entitled to fair treatment and access to comprehensive medical care."

This approach goes over like a lead Zeppelin and Tasha "Taystee" Jefferson responds with "As lady president, I'll demand waterbeds for everybody! We'll be dreamin' like Beyonce on a yacht every night up in here. Comprehensive that, bitches! Yo!"

As the former accountant for Parker's drug operation, Jefferson surely has the mental capacity to understand what Burset is proposing. Why does she work so hard to shoot down a proposal that would benefit all of the prisoners?

It may very well be because Jefferson understands the charade of the prison much better than Burset ever will. Under the *unwritten* rules of the place, the prisoners are entitled to only as many rights and privileges as they can grab using their own resources. Seen in that light, Burset's plea for medical care is as ridiculous as a demand for Figueroa to provide turn-down services, waterbeds, and bedtime stories, because the prisoners lack the power to take those things with their own hands.

But Burset has violated Nietzsche's rules too. In *Thus Spoke Zarathustra,* the philosopher quips "Behold the good and just! Whom do they hate most? Him who breaketh up their tables of values, the breaker, the lawbreaker: he, however, is the creator."

In other words, Burset is the *creator* leading the way to a new system and a new way of thinking for the prisoners at Litchfield, not their victim.

"He who hath to be a creator in good and evil—verily, he hath first to be a destroyer, " Nietzsche teaches us, "and break values in pieces." Burset is doing this every day she draws breath, first by shattering the myth that gender is biologically determined and immutable, second by—to the general befuddlement of Litchfield prisoners and staff—seemingly "choosing" a lesser status as a woman. The fact that Burset had no more had any choice in that decision than Chapman has the capacity not to be annoying goes over the heads of those who observe her.

Thus, when she tries to act like a prisoner, Burset is doomed to failure. When she acts like a *creator*, she makes progress. In Season Two's "A Whole Other Hole," it falls to Burset to enlighten Jefferson's brain trust that urine does not, in fact, come out of one's vagina unless something is seriously wrong and inserting a tampon is actually relatively simple.

"For the love of God, girls the hole is not inside the hole," Burset says "You have your vagina proper, then you have your clitoris. The urethra is located between the clit and the vagina, inside the labia minora."

Of course, none of them believe her until Burset adds "I designed one myself. Had plans drawn up and everything. I've seen some funky punani in my day. I'm not gonna leave that shit up to chance."

Even then, Burset is forced to hand Jefferson—who's sitting on a toilet trying to comprehend the mysteries of tampon insertion—a compact mirror with an invitation to go exploring before she's truly believed.

"Oh my God!" exclaims Jefferson. "Holy shit! *Yo, y'all, she's right!*" (emphasis added).

Notice the pronouns. Not "he-she's right." Not "It's right." She's right. *That's* the moment when things start to change. For the first time, Burset is seen by her peers not as a freak of indeterminate gender, but as a *woman*—indeed, as a woman who knows more about their own bodies than they do.

The epilogue to this at the end of the episode, where Burset runs a more organized lecture on vulval and vaginal geography for women from all of the Litchfield cliques, would be anti-climactic but for the uninvited presence of Officer Scott O'Neill, who is even more ignorant than the prisoners on this subject. His dropped jaw during the scene is worth waiting the entire season for, as is what he does with the newfound knowledge on how to find a clitoris later. He doesn't say anything to Burset, but doesn't really need to—the awe in his eyes is submission enough by a representative of the prison of their newfound respect for Burset.

The lesson in all this? Burset knows this stuff because she *had* to learn it as a trans woman. Acknowledging and honoring that leads her to a place of power over her colleagues and, at least, over O'Neill. While it would tie things up in a nice bow to have Crystal reach a similar realization where Burset is concerned, pat resolutions make for bad television.

The Dialectics of Litchfield

Throughout the first two seasons. Burset's experiences support Nietzsche's conclusion in *Twilight of Idols* that "One chooses dialectics only when one has no other expedient. One knows that dialectics inspire mistrust, that they are not very convincing. Nothing is easier to expunge than the effect of a dialectician, as is proved by the experience of every speech-making assembly."

Think back to "Lesbian Request Denied," where Burset attempts to secure her hormones via rational and logical arguments to the prison and to her spouse—and fails miserably. Or to "WAC Pack", where she gives a variant of the "All we have to lose are our chains" speech and sees it fall on deaf ears.

But in "A Whole Other Hole," Burset doesn't *argue*. Instead, she *acts*. She tells Jefferson where her urethra is—and empowers her (by giving her the mirror) to come to the same conclusion herself. Similarly, she doesn't *ask* Figueroa for permission to give a Female Anatomy 101 class—she just does it. By *asking*, she fails. By *acting*, she succeeds.

It's no coincidence that one of the primary lyrics from the show's theme song, "You've Got Time" by Regina Spektor, is "Taking steps is easy; standing still is hard." The entire prison is set up to get Burset and her colleagues to stand still, since if they can be made to do so, they lose. If they act, they have a chance to win.

That's the lesson of what happens when a nineteenth-century German philosopher meets a twenty-first-century African-American trans woman in an American federal prison. It's a pity Nietzsche is no longer with us—I sense a sequel to *Zarathustra* entitled *Thus Spoke Sophia Burset* would be a fascinating book indeed.

4
It's Different but the Same

Rod Carveth

When she was just twenty-four, Piper Kerman flew to Belgium carrying a suitcase full of cash to a West African drug cartel head kingpin given to her by her heroin-dealing girlfriend. Years later, Kerman was arrested, and later convicted, for felony money-laundering. Kerman served thirteen months in the Danbury, Connecticut, Correctional Institute, and then wrote a book about her experience, which became a bestseller—*Orange Is the New Black*, since adapted as a TV series on Netflix.

The TV show follows the character Piper Chapman as a privileged Smith College alum having to adjust to life in prison. The series has been praised for its critique of the US prison system, as well as its diversity of female characters, yet in has been criticized for its reliance on a privileged white character.

Piper

We can explore the role of African-American characters on *Orange Is the New Black* from the reference point of the predominant white character on the show—Piper Chapman. Piper's an interesting character because she is a well-educated product of a protected upper-middle class background, someone who is socially liberal, but a person who has not had much experience with lower-income women of color. No matter how much she tries, she's an outsider in the environment of Litchfield.

In the episode entitled "WAC Pack," Piper's mother visits and tells her that she is worried over Piper's mental health. Piper retorts, "I am not going crazy. I am surrounded by crazy. And it's like climbing up Mount Everest in flip-flops. But I am not crazy." Piper's mom then claims that Piper is in prison because of what Alex did. "If it wasn't for her, you would be trying on wedding dresses," her mother asserts. In response, Piper declares "I am in here because I am no different than anyone else in here." What Piper is arguing here is that she is no better than her other inmates, and, at the same time, calling out what she sees as her mother's prejudice. Piper then goes on to say that "I made bad choices. I committed a crime. It is nobody's fault that I am in here but mine."

This interaction is instructive because while Piper may seek solidarity with her fellow inmates, her mother is right—Piper's not like the other inmates. She is in a world for which she has no understanding ("I am surrounded by crazy"), and while it's admirable on one level that she's taking responsibility for her actions, she also discounts the racial and economic forces that led to her fellow inmates having a greater probability of serving time. For them, it is not just a matter of making "bad choices." For them, the path into the criminal justice system comes from such circumstances as being severely abused by a boyfriend, being forced into the sex trade, being "persuaded" (willingly or unwillingly) into becoming drug mules, or being forced to commit crimes in order to feed their babies.

There are times that Piper is self-aware enough to know that she is apart from her fellow inmates. When an inmate complains that Piper is "in denial" about the privileges she enjoyed on the outside (and, to some extent, in Litchfield itself), Piper responds, "I'm a WASP. It's [meaning denial] what we do." In addition, Piper is able to use her background to gain favor with Healy, the prison counselor. When in the series first episode, Healy warns Piper to "stay away" from lesbians (ironic because a lesbian relationship contributed to why Piper is in prison), Piper indicates that she is engaged to a man. She lets Healy know this because she wants her fiancé to visit. While she may not have intended it, she also communicates that, like Healy, she is straight, and uncomfortable with homosexuality. Healy thus assumes that her loyalties will be with him over her fellow inmates, and treats her differently than other inmates based on this assumption.

This will work to her favor. In the episode "The Chickening" Healy punishes Poussey Washington, a Black inmate, for running on prison grounds. By contrast, he tells Piper that he won't send her to the SHU (solitary confinement), because she's "new" and just "made a mistake." He warns Piper to avoid exciting the inmates in the future: "They're not like you and me. They're less reasonable. Less educated."

When Healy wants Piper to run for the Women's Advisory Council, he pulls out two different dresses for him to check against her coloring. At first Piper wonders who the dresses are for. Healy tells Piper that they are for his wife's birthday, but the message is clear—she is inside a prison and nice things like those dresses are beyond her reach for now.

Healy then indicates he wants Piper to run for WAC. "We don't get ladies as bright as you very often," he observes. Healy then reveals why he wants Piper to run, "The two of us working together, we could really turn some things around. Or at least, make things a little quieter." Healy does not want the inmates to have too much power, as that will make his job that much harder. Healy sees Piper as an ally (because they have "so much in common"), and less of a challenge to his authority than other inmates. Though Piper declines to run for WAC, preferring to not to stand out too much during her stay at Litchfied, Healy rigs the election so she wins a seat on the WAC.

Healy's preferential treatment of Piper means that, willingly or unwillingly, she's complicit in Healy's goal of making sure the inmates have as little power as possible. More than once Healy will ask, "Chapman, we understand each other, don't we?" and she will respond, "I think so." Though Piper might not consciously acknowledge it, she appears to agree with Healy in that they are "different" (as in better) than the others in Litchfield.

Taystee

Taystee's character perhaps best illustrates the societal barriers the inmates at Litchfield have to face. Taystee grew up not only abandoned, but while at an orphanage was victimized by a predator who acted as a father figure. Vee, a drug dealer, discovered Taystee during an adoption fair. She soon made Taystee the accountant for her drug ring because of Taystee's mathematical skills.

Taystee was reluctant to join the drug business, but realized the most likely alternative for her was flipping burgers. That made it easy for Vee to convince Taystee that dealing drugs would offer her both an income, and a level of respect for her accounting skills. Unfortunately for Taystee, the drug business not only cost Taystee her freedom, but the life of her adoptive brother as well.

When Taystee is released on parole, the first thing she does is look for Vee, who happens to be fleeing from police—only to be arrested and sen to, of all places, Litchfield. With no job, school, or even halfway house options available to her, Taystee has no choice but to deliberately violate her parole, and return to Litchfield. Taystee returns to prison because she has learned a bitter lesson: Litchfield is the only place where she fits in. As she tells her fellow inmates upon her return, at least inside she has a bed, a routine, and friends.

An argument between Piper and Taystee (who is the Black inmates' representative on WAC), shows how different the two are from one another because of their experiences and backgrounds. Piper believes that she can effect real change at Litchfield, particularly in terms of the prison's health care and educational services. Taystee knows better—Healy has no interest in the inmates achieving any real change. He just wants them to be quiet. As a result, Taystee advocates for small items, such as *Fifty Shades of Gray* in the prison library. Taystee knows that the council is basically a sham. When Piper complains that Taystee is breaking her campaign promises, Taystee shrugs, "That's politics."

Sophia

Before transitioning, Sophia Burset was a firefighter named Marcus who was married to a woman named Crystal and had a son, Michael. In order to pay for her sex-reassignment operations, Sophia stole credit cards, boosting them to finance her surgeries. Though Crystal stuck by Sophia as she was transitioning, Michael could not deal with his father becoming a woman. As a result, Michael turned Sophia in to the authorities. Though Sophia has been in prison for two years, Michael has visited Sophia once since her arrest.

Sophia is the most maternal character on *Orange Is the New Black*. She often gives compassionate support to the other prisoners, even though she has to deal with discrimination due to being the only transgender inmate. She is also unwavering in her quest to be the best parent possible for her son, even though he turned her in. In the episode "Fucksgiving," Sophia gets upset during a visit from Crystal when Crystal suggests she has a new man—a pastor—in her life. Sophia protests that she doesn't want another man around her son. Crystal responds, "We don't always get what we want, do we?"

Sophia also gives a powerful face and voice to the problematic imprisonment of transgender individuals and the subsequent mistreatment of them while in prison. The prison attempts to undermine her gender identity through restricted access to essential hormones. As Sophia says, "I don't need to pay for the car. I just need the body oil." Her portrayal shows the viewers the injustice of not being allowed to be who you are.

Sophia is played by Laverne Cox, one of the few transgender actors actually playing a transgender role. From Felicity Huffman as the transgendered woman lead in the 2005 movie *Transamerica*, to Adam Torres in *Degrassi: The Next Generation*, transgender characters have been played by straight actors. Even Amazon's *Transparent* features cisgendered Jeffrey Tambor as the transitioning character.

Cox has used the momentum and success of the character of Sophia to bring public awareness to imprisoned transgender issues. By using the connection that Sophia has made with audiences, Cox has been able to promote awareness of the essentially invisible issue of transgender imprisonment, with the hope of ultimately changing prison policy.

Portrayal of African Americans on TV

Compared with earlier depictions of minorities in TV shows, *Orange Is the New Black* shows progress, but still conveys some harmful stereotypes.

The term "stereotype" was coined by Walter Lippmann in his famous book, *Public Opinion*, to refer to the "pictures" people hold in their heads. Lippmann's definition served as the foundation for social scientists' concept of stereotypes as overgeneralized mental representations of social groups formed through contact experiences. Positive contact experiences are assumed to promote positive stereotyping, while negative contact experiences result in negative stereotyping. When opportunities for direct contact with racial group members are lacking, the media serve as important agents in the formation and reinforcement of racial stereotypes.

Media research has shown that as individuals are exposed to stereotypical portrayals of racial groups through TV, individuals acquire stereotypes that are similar to the ways the groups are portrayed. The cumulative portrayals of African Americans on television have an influence on viewers and their perceptions about African Americans in general. These negative portrayals often lead to the continuation of stereotypes of African Americans in general. When first-hand knowledge of African Americans is not available, television images have a significant effect on viewers' perceptions. These stereotypes are a problem when they not only reinforce differences among social groups, they also reinforce the social order and its power imbalances.

Content analyses of television reveal that African Americans represent less than one-sixth of the characters of prime time (8–11 P.M.) television. By contrast, whites represent about four-fifths of the characters. Blacks are usually featured in two genres of television programming—situation comedies and crime drama. The typical African American on prime time is a male in his thirties. African-American males are often shown as being clowns, brutes, pimps, "oreo," "homo thugs," and absentee fathers.

African-American women were essentially relegated to situation comedies until the 1990s (with the exception of the short-lived action series, *Get Christy Love*). Things began to change in the 1990s, with the crime series *Homicide: Life on the Streets*, and today, African-American women are in leading roles in some of the most popular TV series, such as *Scandal* and *Empire*. Still, African-American female characters have been routinely portrayed as "the mammy," the "jezebel," the "welfare queen," and "the angry black woman."

African Americans portrayed on television are generally depicted in service or blue-collar occupations, such as a servant, cook, entertainer, musician, or athlete. African Americans are seldom depicted as having a professional or supervisory position in comparison to white television characters.

Many African Americans have negative personality characteristics such as being disrespectful, violent, greedy, ignorant, and power-driven. African Americans have lower socioeconomic status (SES) roles on television than whites, as well as possessing lower educational levels. Most importantly, African Americans are over-represented as criminals on television compared to white characters.

Still a Ways to Go

Though the portrayals of Taystee and Sophia are multidimensional and avoid many of the stereotypes seen in other portrayals of characters of color, there are also aspects of *Orange Is the New Black* that reinforce previous stereotypes. For example, the show conveys the message that a number of society's ills are caused by low-income African-American women being poor parents. Vee, who took in Taystee in a presumed maternal role, instead sadistically preys upon the discarded and ignored children of her 'hood, directing them into drug dealing. Vee may function as their mother, but she will also order their executions if they cross her.

In addition, consider also how *Orange Is the New Black* depicts being punished with solitary confinement. At Litchfield, inmates who commit serious transgressions are sent to the "Shoe" (SHU or special housing unit). When Piper is confined to the SHU for dancing too provocatively with Alex, the viewers are shown that such confinement is a serious matter. In the real world, human rights organizations have declared that solitary confinement is a form of torture, one meted out with a lack of due process. Inmates are often sent to solitary confinement by guards and administrations who do not concern themselves with judicial review. Healy sends Piper to SHU even though prison guard Pablo says that he likely has no grounds to.

Yet, the only time viewers see anyone suffering from their time in the SHU is when Piper is sentenced there. While the SHU has a revolving door for Black women and Latinas, the show only focuses on Piper's painful experience there. It is as if their suffering doesn't count.

In the episode "WAC Pack," there is a scene that highlights common stereotypes among the inmates. Over in the white inmates' area of the cafeteria, Lorna declares that "Hispanics . . . live like twenty people to one apartment, they have more kids than even the Irish . . . they're dirty, they're greasy, and they're taking our jobs." Meanwhile, at a Latina table, the group observes that African Americans are "smelly, stupid, and lazy, but they ain't got different bones"—'cept in their pants." Meanwhile, at the African-American table, Taystee and Poussey riff on "white people politics," decrying white upper-class dilettantism (from yoga to veganism), sexual repression ("quiet sex every night at nine o'clock"), and affluence ("Did you hear that piece on NPR about hedge funds?"). These conversations suggest that each of these groups are equally engaged in the same kind of prejudiced stereotyping—the same kind of stereotypes often praised on television.

Therein lies the problem of *Orange Is the New Black* when it comes to African-American portrayals. The series essentially frames the reasons why African American women are in prison as "bad choices" that have their origins in a culture of poverty (as with Taystee) or from behavioral deviance (as with "Crazy Eyes"). The series does not go below the surface to discuss how the inmates Piper encounters are victims of a system that gives them virtually no options for survival, let alone upward mobility, than by engaging in criminal behavior.

At its heart, *Orange Is the New Black* is a fish out of water story about a privileged white woman serving a short-term prison sentence. While the show does provide more multidimensionality to its African American characters than other series on television, the voice of the show is still a white voice. It will be a long time before there is a similar fish-out-of-water story about an African-American woman in prison, maybe because for both television and real life, prison *is* the water.

III

Every day in this place I get more confused

5
Prison Is Hell

CHRISTOPHER KETCHAM

When Piper Kerman self-surrenders at the penitentiary, she's greeted at the door by the ghost of Jeremy Bentham. She doesn't see this specter, of course, but he sees her and grimaces.

"Another one who could have benefited from my beloved panopticon," the philosopher muses to himself. But nearly two hundred years after Bentham conceived his way of improving the British workhouse, it, and the idea of the prison have somehow been transmogrified into the maw that leads down into Dante's inferno: Hell itself. And the sign above the modern prison should read, "Beware Who Enter Here that All Dignity Will Be Stripped from You and Not Ever Returned."

Even on your last day when there is no more reason to punish you, you will be punished and this punishment will never leave you, for it has marked your psyche forever. Remember Roland (in the book, not the TV show)? Her parents showed up on Roland's last day in a different car than was registered on her paperwork. They were sent away and Roland was kept two more weeks. . . . In the correctional system everyone, even your family, is punished.

THIS LETTER WAS SENT BY AN INMATE WHO IS IN A STATE PRISON. THE STATE IS NOT RESPONSIBLE FOR DEBTS INCURRED OR FOR THE CONTENTS OF THE LETTER.

Congratulations, you have a relative in prison. You never know what the letter will say because you don't know what's happening to him. Unlike Piper, most probably he's a he and, again unlike Piper, he's probably in a state prison. He's not a camper like Piper but in a 'real' prison, high security. He's not in lockdown or wasn't when he wrote the letter. But letters sometimes are few and far between because he gets sent to solitary far too often and loses letter-writing privileges. One time they mailed all his belongings home in a box with no note or anything. You thought he was dead. You called. Inmate privacy, they said, can't say anything more, click. So he wasn't dead. But he was in a six-months-long twenty-four hour lockdown for some bogus rules infraction, or so he said, when a letter finally did come.

He, your relative, wants money, always needs money in the form of an expensive money order (just like Piper) you purchase with your own money and send to the commissary because the food the prison serves is basically inedible. He will spend it on prepared foods sealed in plastic and other things like the letter paper and envelope, some of it to consume, some for favors to pay debts, and even for protection against the gangs that own the prison, inside the walls.

Or he will trade goods for drugs or some alcohol concoction made from fruit or rice. He'll pay too much for the food because, well, the prison has him captive remember, and they can charge him whatever they can get that you will pay for. And the letter will be handwritten, probably one of the few hand-written letters you will ever expect to receive in today's world of e-mails, Twitter, and Facebook. If he's been in long enough, he probably doesn't know any of these social media platforms or if he has heard about them what he has heard is probably distorted. You don't take his reverse-the-charges, person-to-person, operator-assisted prison payphone calls anymore because they're too expensive. Not like Piper's PAC number which charged her prison account from the money order she got regularly from Larry. In most state prisons the most expensive phone call option is used and you, the relative, pay for it. I know, either way the relative pays.

And you remember the time you got on the visitation list the required week ahead of time and drove three hours one way only to be told he had been put into lockdown an hour after you called. Nobody called to let you know his visitation rights had been cancelled. You're *his* relative; who cares? He's just inmate scum and you as his relative probably are as well. And you recall the time you made the drive with your sister who dressed very well but when you got there they told her her skirt was too tight. She had to wait in the car while you visited alone. And in that waiting room with all the relatives of murderers and rapists and drug dealers you were dressed comfortably but put on some expensive perfume to smell nice for your relative. Then a trusty came into the waiting room and sprayed Lysol over everything and everyone.

Someone said that the inmates believe that the dogs can't smell drugs over the scent. But that's just prison legend. Sure, you get a sanitized view of the prison, the waiting room, some hallways, and the visitation room. You don't get to see what really goes on inside. Odds are very good you have a relative or a friend, or a college or work chum or even a neighbor, maybe two, maybe more, who is doing or has done time. So, how'd it get so bad?

Hey, Jeremy, WTF?

Jeremy Bentham believed that we're subject to two masters—pain and pleasure. Utilities are those properties of any object that produce benefit, advantage, pleasure, good, or happiness or prevent the happening of mischief, pain, evil, or unhappiness (*An Introduction*, p. 15). Given our druthers we would like to have as much utility as possible, which, of course, is as much happiness as possible. So the right action out of all the alternatives is the one that produces the most good. This includes not only the actions of people, but the actions of government.

Happiness is always better than unhappiness. And, happiness counts the same for every person, rich or poor. The greater good (happiness) for the greater number trumps everything. So, why do we have a lot of very poor people and a few really rich people? Well, some people need more utility to gain and keep up their happiness quota. There is quite a bit of egoism in Bentham's utilitarianism.

So how does this relate to Piper, you ask? Well, certainly she had some fun in her early days of being involved with Nora (Nora is called "Alex," on the television show) and in drug trafficking. However, it isn't only Piper who determines utility. So does the state. The federal government asked, hmmm, what's the greater good here . . . that Piper Kerman should be happy, or . . . but there is no or—she created a lot more unhappy people by enabling their addiction (the addicts might disagree of course, because the greater the high the greater their happiness, at least for the moment). "Sorry Piper," said the government, "but *your* utility gain is much less than the utility lost to the victims of your crime, so you must be stopped."

Certainly the government could have shown up on her doorstep and said, Hey, don't do this anymore (like your mother would). And, you know what?, Piper would probably have said, "Sure thing!" and have stopped. But another in her place might have nodded and smiled and gone right on doing it. So, the federal cure to the greater unhappiness quotient is to put Piper in an unhappy place, the federal prison, for as long a time as the government thinks her reduction of society's utility should cost her—about fifteen months. And it's worse for the addicts when they get caught because in its infinite wisdom Congress has instituted long mandatory sentences for drug-related offenses. The only way you can get your heroin habit rehabilitated in Danbury is if your sentencing judge says you can, and then you're uprooted from your cushy camper digs for a nine-month stint in the Big House, the high security part of the complex with all of the real psychos and serial killers. . . . But most addicts are like Danbury inmate Allie B. who can't wait to get out to score some junk.

In 2008, The National Institute on Drug Abuse found relapse rates similar to chronic diseases and recommended that drug addiction be treated like a disease. Stick that in your infirmary Federal Correctional Institution in Danbury (NIDA 2008).

Okay, but listen, pull one Piper or a Nora or an Aliaj off the streets and there are ten more waiting in line to dispense more 'happy-unhappiness' in the form of drugs. Right you are, but Bentham would say, "Piper you should have done this happiness calculation yourself." If Piper were a moral person she would have recognized that the right thing to do was to 'Just Say No' to money laundering for the drug trade. But of course, we know the story—she just kind of naively fell into it and couldn't seem to extract herself from it. Besides, her friend Nora ratted on her.

So, what about the rat factor? Does the greater happiness go to the rat or the ratted on? Come now, you've seen enough crime dramas to know that the rat gets the reduced sentence and the ratted on gets hit with the stiffer sentence. Okay, Bentham, explain that with your happiness quotient! "Oh, that isn't so hard," he might say, "the state is happier because it has a lot less work to do (keeps more utility) and probably will have an easier time and cost the many taxpayers much less prosecuting the case, so credit the rat with the greater happiness in society." The scales of justice and happiness simply tipped away from Piper.

But why make the relatives of the prisoners suffer long waits, lack of information, the expense of decent inmate meals, and other ridiculous inconveniences? Shouldn't the prison staff be punished for taking away the innocent relatives' happiness, decreasing their utility? Oh, well, maybe they just didn't get the memo. Besides, the law trumps happiness doesn't it? But that's just the thing. The political motivation behind Bentham's utilitarian approach to happiness was to rid the world of bad laws that lacked utility. Jeremy Bentham's rolling in his grave. Well, not really, as we'll find out later.

Is Everybody Happy?

Bentham saw two kinds of people in this world. The first seek to maximize pleasure in *this* world and as a result try to avoid pain. Others seek to avoid the pain of a vengeful God and do right just to be certain that the hot pokers of Hell will not impale them (*An Introduction*, p. 20). So which one are you, the pious aesthete who prays and tithes the church and avoids all sorts of pleasures in this life to have your pleasure in what is purported to be a very long afterlife? Or are you the glutton, the hoarder, the addict who needs more and more—the would-be billionaire, amassing the greater fortune at the expense of the little people who have little or no fortune? Some people just need more utility (money, food, drugs) to reach the happy threshold, don't they? Certainly Piper isn't the religious type, but is she a glutton?

So you begin to see the dilemma here. Just what is utility and how do you measure goodness? In whose eyes is goodness calculated? The child of the billionaire is not happy. "What's there to do in this overblown dump? Oh, I'm so bored." She needs more to make her happy, doesn't she? So while happiness is measured the same between people, for some, much more of the much more is the cure for unhappiness. . . . Like, it now takes five OxyContins to get me high.

Greed Is Good!

Piper got busted because the government said she created more unhappiness by enabling addicts' addictions. And we all know that addicts steal for a fix and drug dealers kill to protect their turf, and so on, and so on, yadda yadda.

However, the billionaire developer in Boston (far away from the nice digs Piper grew up in) has just evicted two thousand poor apartment dwellers in a gentrifying section of town. Not only is he awarded significant tax abatements for his new luxury condos; he's given awards and accolades by the city for his civic-mindedness and beautification efforts. Certainly we can't be saying that all people are equal but some people are more equal than others! Why not? Who calculates happiness? Um, the city in this case. The new condos even with tax abatements will generate significantly more revenue for the city because the two thousand happy wealthy new tenants will spend, spend, spend, . . . and besides, those two thousand unhappy apartment dwellers, well they were just a drag on our entire economy. Only makes sense, doesn't it? Apartment dwellers, find your own happiness. It's your job!

What?

"Hey," Bentham would probably respond, "we only should do things to increase *our* happiness. That's all that matters" . . . Well, he later begrudgingly made an exception for the philanthropist . . . but even then the philanthropist gets something out of it. "Wait, my philanthropy *has* improved the lives of people in Third-worldland. . . . And they're starting to buy my computers. Everyone's happy now, right?"

Here We Go 'Round the Panopticon, the Panopticon, the Panotpicon

Morals reformed—health preserved—industry invigorated instruction diffused—public burthens lightened—Economy seated, as it were, upon a rock—the Gordian knot of the Poor-Laws are not cut, but untied—all by a simple idea in Architecture!

So wrote Jeremy Bentham of his epiphany, *The Panopticon or the Inspection House* composed as a series of letters to a friend in 1787. His grand vision would eliminate the need for the poorhouse and cut the costs of administering justice through his brilliant redesign—the round penitentiary.

The panopticon was guaranteed to reduce the cost of incarceration and reduce recidivism, but at what cost? Was prison necessary for Piper? Probably not, she just wasn't cut out to be a drug mule and she knew it. She served her time and went home. So far so good. But odds are that most others will return to prison. (The Bureau of Justice Statistics reported in 2014 that a study done between 2005 and 2010 in thirty states found three of four who were released from prison returned or violated their terms of release.)

The panopticon is the model of efficiency. Contrast it with Piper's messy corridor-ridden open dormitory style Federal Correctional Institutional campground.

First, build a circular outer concrete or stone wall of say five or six stories and space windows evenly apart. Then build an inner wall to normal prison cell length, install a cell door and close off the cell side walls in the usual manner with concrete walls. Cover the roof and make it secure from escape. Of course, make the cell door bars from steel and bar the outside windows but let the light of the day from the window shine through the barred prison door. Now, go to the center of the building. It's empty, you see, because all you built were walls and a roof so the thing looks like a kettle turned upside down.

It's an inspection house. So, let's inspect. In the center of the open building construct a round tower tall enough to see into the highest cell and put a guard tower on the top with louvered windows or, if you prefer, a one way mirror, mirror side out. Now fill the panopticon's cells with prisoners and put one guard in the tower. The guard can see the silhouette of every prisoner in every cell, but the prisoners can't see the guard. Convenient, low cost, efficient, and keeps escapes to a minimum because every con is always in view. Certainly, put a light in each cell for the evening shift guard. Let a few prisoners at any one time exercise in the empty space below the tower. No prisoner is *ever* out of sight of the tower.

The idea of the panopticon was mind control. The psychology of the panopticon is simple. The prisoner feels naked and unsure whether the guard is looking at her or him or not. Even if the guard should decide to take a short catnap, who but the guard knows that he's sleeping? Everything a prisoner does is subject to inspection (the five times a day count Piper experienced is much easier in the panopticon because all you're looking for are empty cells).

The always-under-surveillance prisoner becomes paranoid, then angry, and eventually numb in the sheer boredom of the place but is hyper-vigilant of the ever-watching eye. Infractions are immediately seen and dealt with. And to make the world even more naked, the prisoner can also see bodies in about half of the cells of the round; where they appear like little ants or bees and sometimes the prisoner can imagine what others are doing and sometimes not.

Punishment Is an Evil

Punishment is an evil. So said Bentham in his *Rationale of Punishment* (p. 1). Wait a minute. Here we have Bentham writing chapter and verse about how great it is to be happier than happy, but then he designs what he considered to be the ultimate prison . . . and following that he says that punishment is an evil? How does this hang together? (No pun intended).

Well, remember the panopticon isn't really a torture chamber. It's a replacement for the workhouse—and its utility comes from the fact that it costs less, enabling the good people of England to keep more of their money (utility: happiness). The British workhouse was a place where the destitute could live and pay for their room and board by working. It was like a prison for the homeless. And the workhouse-cum-panopticon is a place where industry can get goods made cheaply which means more happiness money for the captains of industry.

But what about the prisoners, you ask? Ah but there is more than enough happiness to go around for all, including the prisoners. They learn and practice a useful trade and earn a bit for themselves. Second, they learn the rules on what happiness means, and how obeying the laws, while it is not a ticket to happiness, certainly is a solution against the unhappiness of incarceration. But why didn't Piper know this about rules? Certainly she knew this. She came from a good family and graduated from Smith College.

But there's more. The design of the panopticon also enables the happiness of salvation! "You see," paraphrasing Bentham, "the continuous round building where prisoners are confined when they are not working, eating or exercising is convenient for the clergy to visit one by one without missing a soul, all in order to set each one on the right path towards their eternal reward."

You're putting me on. Nope, Bentham has your earthly life and eternal life covered. Think of it, the Feds would have saved the not-so-happy taxpayers a lot of money as well if Piper wasn't in the Danbury Country Club but in the Danbury panopticon where she could learn a new manual trade and be spiritually saved.

No, there wasn't a lot of 'saving' going on at Danbury. But what new trade did Piper learn in this modern-day penitentiary? Changing light bulbs. Wasn't this menial task simply punishment and as a result, an evil? Well, you can say that. And you would be right because you see, the state has come to see that pun-

ishment is more important than work for those who
don't obey the law. Those who don't obey the law are
put into prison, a kind of warehouse, where they lose
all their freedoms and most of their rights and are expected to rigorously obey strict rules. Those who do
not follow the prison rules get even more punishment.
Following rules—any rules (good or bad), laws, regulations, and other mandates (in prison or out) produces happiness by not bringing on punishment. But
isn't that backwards?

Who the Hell Is Jeremy Bentham and Why Is He Staring at Me Like That?

Upon his death, Bentham ordered his skeleton and
head to be preserved as an auto icon—his skeleton
was stuffed with straw and covered with the dress of
the day and his preserved head was mounted on top
of his seated frame. He stares out from his post-
mortem prison cell in public view at University College, London. His panopticon also has been entombed.
While he peddled the idea to leaders and legislators
across England, no one took him up on the idea and
not a single round inspection house was built. But his
ideas were adopted in other ways: solitary; lame
prison work; control of masses; separation and segre-
gation; boredom . . .

Bentham was adamant, "So, if they are incarcerated
why not get them work and work in ways they can or
would like to perform a useful transferable trade? Certainly this will give them something profitable to do
and will provide them with skills they can use on the
outside. And think of the boost to the economy from
having the prisoners work! License contractors who

will supply necessary work and tax them accordingly. And encourage the prisoners to work, and if they will not, confine them to their cells."

Hitler thought that the prison contractor was a brilliant idea and he used it to build his arsenal of war. . . . If they wouldn't work they were killed; if they did work they starved to death. . . . Hitler's idea of prison food was even worse than most prisons today. But Bentham wasn't into beating or killing the prisoners. He built disincentives like fines and the like into his hypothetical contractor's agreements for injuries and worse.

But what's happened to this idea of useful occupations? Well, at Danbury there's the puppy program to train dogs, and Unicor which makes radio components for the military. There's cooking and cleaning in the prison cafeteria (like Pop, Piper's roommate)—perfect for a minimum wage fast food occupation on the outside. Janet and Piper got the electric shop—where they spent time changing light bulbs in government houses. But this is Danbury Country Club, campers. Just a few yards away in the Big House prisoners learn from each other how to better their skills in jacking cars, dealing drugs, or operating extortion rackets. The prisoner-to-prisoner occupation exchange is without bounds.

The Economical Edge

The design of the panopticon produces economies by reducing the number of guards that are necessary. Since the prisoners are in full view at all times, escape attempts can be caught quickly. As a result, walls do not have to be so sturdy or thick (saves cost). The contracted work returns revenue to offset the cost of housing the prisoners. There can be central heating and a central communications system. Keeping prisoners occupied produces useful fatigue and leaves them less time to engage in nefarious practices.

Today prison work is a perk. At FCI Connecticut it's a perk for the most trustworthy, those who submit without complaint to every regulation and rule. Those given work ostensibly refrain from gang activities, though guards can be bribed. In Danbury most of the work just gives the prisoner something to do; with the exception of dog trainer, it doesn't necessarily provide much experience that's valuable on the outside.

In men's prisons, learning how to be a good gang member certainly provides the inmate with a more useful and lucrative prospect of employment on the outside, though life expectancy is considerably less. But think of all the drug highs, money, and excitement of carrying and using a high powered weapon to enforce your happiness! That's what many of today's prisoners have to look forward to on the outside. On the inside, they protect their turf and use sharpened toothbrush handles as shivs to administer their twisted codes of conduct and to maintain appropriate punishments and retributions as required by their unwritten rules. Piper was lucky. She was smart, a woman, and in the federal minimum-security pen. Not a true country club for sure, but not a concentrated stew of explosive gangs ready to boil over.

So why don't we reconsider the panopticon? Wouldn't it help people learn useful skills that are in demand on the outside, we could lower the cost of guarding prisoners, and possibly even reduce the influence of gangs? "Nope, we need to talk tough, act tough about crime," says the legislator, "especially non-violent crime involving evil drugs."

Drugs are evil. Prison is punishment for drugs. Punishment is evil. Hell is evil. Prison is hell. Hell isn't for sissies. Nuff said.

6
Hell Is Other People but Mostly You Too

COURTNEY NEAL

Piper Chapman is a clearly defined—if annoying—character, with a clear vision of what her time in prison will be. She's going to read a ton of books and get in really good shape, but once inside, Piper is confronted not only with an unexpected group of women and guards, but also herself.

The WASPy but rebellious Piper tries desperately to maintain her external life while in prison, including her engagement with Larry and her new business with Polly through visits and phone calls, but the fishbowl of prison life overtakes Piper before long. The Piper who went into prison though is different from the Piper inside. Her loss of freedom doesn't just impact her external life, but it changes who she is as a person too.

Locked Up

Jean-Paul Sartre's famous play *No Exit* deals with three terrible people who are locked in a room together for eternity in their perfectly calibrated hell. The punishment isn't terrible torture or fire and brimstone, but each other. Each character wants something from the other (love and redemption), but the object of their hope despises them on an extremely personal level. The vicious circle binds the trio together as they all hope to find solace, but they seek it from someone incapable of providing it.

Sartre explored how confinement with others, especially those who have something you need but can't get and whom you also despise, can be punishment all by itself, more so then any physical discomfort.

Litchfield is hardly personalized to that degree, but the isolation of prison, combined with Piper's fellow inmates, has a direct impact on her perception of herself. Piper's priorities begin to change, and old habits return, most clearly through her rekindled relationship with her ex-girlfriend Alex Vause, who is also the person who ratted her out to the cops.

Alex both agonizes and galvanizes Piper, much like the trio in Sartre's play. Alex was her rebellion, and she never felt more alive than when she was with her; however Alex is also the reason Piper's in prison, further complicating their dysfunctional relationship. When Larry lies and says Alex didn't rat Piper out, the two resume their relationship, further messing with Piper and ultimately destroying her engagement with Larry. This conflict with Alex mirrors the debate and trouble of *No Exit* as Piper both wants redemption with Alex, but needs to punish her as well. Despite this anger, the two can't reconcile to only hating or only loving the other, but oscillate between the two, like when Piper yells, "I love you and I fucking hate you" ("Fool Me Once"). Being locked up isn't the worst part of prison, but it's the other inmates, especially Alex, that make prison the hell that it is.

Reciprocated Affection

Alex, though Piper's main source of torment and affection, is not the only shaping force in Piper's time at Litchfield. Piper makes new friends (though almost exclusively in her own white tribe), but the women are completely different then her WASPy network and even the cultured, jet-setting group she met while Alex's girlfriend. Despite her friendships with Nicky and Morello, it's Alex who is at the center of Piper's prison world. The need for attachment and affection is heightened in prison, as seen in the importance of prison families and the intense relationships the women develop with each other.

Brook Soso, though still relatively new to prison and a version of Piper when she first arrived, realizes this need for sisterhood, and even though it's not the grand idea she had hoped for, she never gives up in trying to create connections rather then continue to fight. When Pennsatucky and her old friends are falling out in the laundry room (again), Soso snaps, saying, "Everyone in this place is sad and mad. I mean I get it, we're in prison, it sucks. But we should be leaning on each other, finding support in our fellow criminals so we're not isolated. I need a friend" ("We Have Manners, We're Polite"). The importance of both emotional and physical affection is clear, and the lack of it is often one of the strongest driving forces in exacerbating the ladies' unhappiness. Interpersonal relationships are clearly just as punishing in Litchfield as they are for Sartre, but an even bigger factor for both the inmates and Sartre is the acknowledgement of truth.

The Truth Will Make You Her Bitch

Without worldly distractions (except for the meager ones available in prison), Piper and the other characters are left with ample time for self-reflection and to analyze the question, "How the hell did I end up here?" The flashbacks serve to provide an additional window into the backstory of featured characters, but revelations in prison serve to create a new truth, as everyone, but new arrivals especially, begin to see who they really are without any distractions.

In *No Exit* each character must reveal their terrible deeds and personality traits that have condemned them, and this knowledge serves to both alienate them from each other, and make them further despise themselves. Just as the contrary personality types punish the inmates, their personal explorations can result in unpleasant histories and habits to be not only made public, but directly dealt with.

In "Bora Bora Bora" a "Scared Straight!" demonstration comes to Litchfield. Some of the ladies are extremely excited to take part and revel in their ability to play the part of hardened inmates. Suzanne, a.k.a. Crazy Eyes, chooses to recite Shakespearean verse— which makes her seem even more crazy to the girls— while the other ladies stick to a more traditional script of "Scared Straight!" programs. The ladies play their parts from the beginning, with the sole goal to maximize the scare tactics of the program, regardless of the truth of Litchfield's day-to-day operation. Suzanne's bow after her monologue further shows that this is a performance by the ladies, that they realize this isn't really what prison is, but that it's necessary to try and turn the girls around. When simply yelling at and intimidating the girls isn't enough, the inmates show off the disgusting bathroom. This seems to work on everyone except Dina, the wheelchair bound thug who seems emptier than anyone in Litchfield.

Dina's hardened attitude is a dead end for Poussey and the others, but when Piper turns up, they try to get her to achieve what they themselves haven't been able to do. They continue in the same vein, asking Piper to regale the girls with tales of how terrifying the communal bathroom is and describe predatory lesbianism, but Piper remains oblivious to their purpose. When Piper still doesn't realize the others want her to play along, Dina laughs at the realization, "Oh man, this is a joke, you all just puttin' on a show." For Dina, the physical condition of prison and even the threat of other actions are irrelevant and met with a persistent declaration that "I don't care" and "Whatever." The main group leaves Dina behind with Piper out of frustration, and Piper genuinely tries to turn Dina straight with kind words, but is appalled at her disgust when she touches her shoulder. This break in her armor leads Piper to deliver a long monologue that, unlike the others, relies on the truth of prison life, and directly reveals to us exactly what her time in Litchfield has done to her:

> **PIPER:** You know I could tell you a lot of things that would scare you, Dina. I could tell you that I'm going to make you my prison bitch. I could tell you that I'm going to make you my house mouse, that I will have sex with you even if we don't have an emotional connection; that I'm going to do to you what the spring does with cherry trees but in a prison way. Pablo Neruda. But why bother? You're too tough, right? Yeah, I know how easy it is to convince yourself that you're something you're not. I mean you could do that on the outside. You can just keep moving, keep yourself so busy you don't have to face who you really are. But you're weak.

DINA: Back the fuck off me.

PIPER: I'm like you Dina. I'm weak too. I can't get through this without somebody to touch, without somebody to love. Is that because sex numbs the pain or is it because I'm some evil fuck monster? I don't know. But I do know that I was somebody before I came in here. I was somebody with a life that I chose for myself and now, now it's just about getting through the day without crying. And I'm scared. I'm still scared. I'm scared that I'm not myself in here and I'm scared that I am. Other people aren't the scariest part of prison Dina. It's coming face-to-face with who you really are. Because once you're behind these walls there's nowhere to run, even if you could run. The truth catches up with you in here Dina and it's the truth that's going to make you her bitch.

Afterwards Piper walks out to see the shocked faces of the other women and girls, and when they say how cold that was, Piper shrugs and says "Bitches got to learn." Piper focuses on the need for affection and connection, while stressing that all the companionship inside still doesn't change the fact that in prison you have to confront who you really are (which for Piper is weak) without any distractions. This hits home for Dina and the others as well, though none more so than Piper.

Piper has reached a level of self-awareness that mirrors the conclusion of *No Exit*, when the trio is forced to confront their own misdeeds, terrible personalities, as well as the lack of hope for redemption. Piper has started to realize that prison is actively changing her, but not in the way she expected: prison is merely showing Piper her true self.

Self-Awareness Should Be a Good Thing

Existentialism advocates self-awareness and the belief that life has no meaning except that which we give to it. It stresses that authenticity is necessary to grasp human existence, and through this you can begin to understand yourself and your place in the world. Without the distractions of the outside world Piper cannot lie or pretend to be something she is not. Her fellow inmates live with her constantly and therefore begin to really know who Piper is, which they have no qualms about constantly reminding and telling her. When she insults Red's cooking during her first week, apologies mean nothing and simply saying she's a nice person does nothing for Piper. For the first time in her life, Piper can't hide from her actions or dismiss them, but must address them daily and directly.

In Litchfield Piper has to confront not only why she has done the things she has, but who she is because of them. As Piper tells Dina, "I'm scared that I'm not myself in here and I'm scared that I am." Without her freedom, Piper cannot distract herself. Early in the show in "The Chickening" Piper tries to hold onto her old ways, taking tea outside to read beneath a tree and snack, but she spots the chicken, setting off the prison-wide obsession with finding it. This is the moment when Piper realizes she is different in prison, with different priorities, and she can't pretend otherwise anymore.

A Prison Isn't Just Walls

Losing her freedom isn't the only punishment in prison, but the self-directed focus on herself wasn't something Piper was anticipating, and is therefore the hardest on her. Piper loses everything she had when she went into prison by the end of the second season: she and Larry have broken up, Polly and Larry are together, and Piper has no business to go back to when she gets out. Piper undergoes an existential crisis and realizes her WASPy nature is no longer the person she is, but neither is the rebellious free spirit of her early twenties. Through extensive self-reflection Piper is beginning to discover her true identity, one that she is quite troubled by. For Sartre, engagement in the world alienates you from your authentic possibility; going to prison then removes the distraction of the world and allows for this critical self-reflection to occur. This is not necessarily a bad thing, the fully examined life, many philosophers would argue, isn't worth living, but for Piper it has rocked her foundation.

Life in prison has forced Piper's path towards authenticity, and the path to it is difficult. Piper will begin to have meaning in her life, but it is still developing. Shedding her inauthentic former life opens the path to create authenticity, however, while Piper is still at Litchfield she does not have complete freedom, therefore she can't become a fully authentic person. The walls of Litchfield close Piper up internally just as much as they separate her from the outside world. Despite these confines Piper's existential crisis and her rocky attempts at both validation and reciprocated affection lead her to examine how much she effects her own happiness and identity.

The walls of Litchfield and physical isolation from friends and family is the punishment that Piper expected when she began to serve her time, but this was not the only punishment she received. As Sartre's trio shows, punishment can be delivered by interacting with others who withhold necessary affection and validation, but self-realization itself is another bitter pill to swallow. Piper feels she has become a new person in prison, but she is also becoming a more authentic. She can no longer hide behind her job, engagement, or being busy to avoid looking at who she is, but the necessity of self-reflection is forced on her in Litchfield. For Piper, her lack of freedom isn't the only way Litchfield is punishing her. The inmates and her time to think are doing that as well.

IV

I'm a predator, bitch. Ain't no fun if you offer

7
Prison as Rehab?
Foucault Says No, No, No

JEFFREY E. STEPHENSON AND SARA WALLER

We're addicted to the TV series *Orange Is the New Black*. The tensions created in the prison by the varied interests and personalities of the characters, prisoners, guards, prison administration, or family members, not to mention the successful use of backstories to propel the developing subplots, together generate a delightful anticipation of what will unfold in the next episode, and then the next, and the next.

However, something about the show began to bother us. We came to recognize that we disliked the main character, Piper Chapman, even though it's her unfolding story that we tune in to watch! This disparity between our enjoyment of the series and dislike of the main character gave us pause: How could we account for the enthusiasm we experienced about the show itself when contrasted with our growing disenchantment with Piper?

Pied Piper

One of the objections to Piper that surfaced was that she's boring and yet she lacks the conviction of will that boring people frequently lack. Unlike the woman whose strained lyric titles this chapter, Piper actually accepts the arbitrarily established values of the class and society into which she's born. This is evidenced in the fact that after posing as a drug money runner (as in, she is a poser), she returns to the soft, safe upper-middle class vanilla world from whence she came, and even assumes that her belonging to that world will protect her from the consequences of her adventures in the rocky road world of heroin trade and drug money transport.

Why? Why is her character packaged in such a humdrum, uninteresting manner? One explanation is that Piper *must* be sympathetically drawn, which is to say, she has to be drawn in such a way that most members of the viewing audience will be able to identify with her. After all, we all enjoy being safe, both socially and financially, and we all like to break some rules occasionally, feel the thrill, and hope to not get caught. If Piper had any depth to her—if she were a more complex character from the margins of society, like Red or Sophia— we might have a far more interesting, authentic narrative, but almost certainly a far less saleable one as well. Instead, to establish a steady viewership for the show and thus maintain its *marketability*, we have the increasingly tiresome and privileged Piper parading her woe-is-me all over our television screens. Like the pied piper of legend, Piper lulls viewers into a somnambulic trance, drawing them into her narrative with bright blue eyes and handmade, scented soap.

Of Blindness to Blandness and Prison

This observation about Piper and the connection to economic considerations got us thinking about broader, more vital issues that the TV series works to conceal, whether intentionally or not; as Freud revealed, we are often not aware of what motivates us. Likewise, narratives frequently omit comprehension of what is being conveyed at some higher level. Perhaps it is a case of not being able to see the forest for the trees.

Could the prison setting represented in the series be a microcosm of the entire structure of power in which viewers of the show are a part? Could our initial blindness to the blandness of Piper, subsequently interpreted as a necessary condition for the show's economic success, be somehow intimately connected to the prison environment in which Piper finds herself?

It's easy to forget that prisons and imprisonment have histories, that their reasons for being and their functions have changed over time. The very fact of incarceration is so much a part of modern day-to-day life that most of us hardly give the genesis of the prison a second thought, let alone speculate on the less obvious functions prisons might serve.

One contemporary reconsideration and interpretation of the function of prisons and imprisonment is provided by Michel Foucault in his book *Discipline and Punish*. For Foucault, the purpose of prison isn't to rehabilitate people to refocusing their energies and attitudes on some mysterious and unspecified "wholesome value system" that will bring them a good life. It isn't to make people better in any abstract sense. Prisons and imprisonment are a crucial part of the modern system of State power, in which all day-to-day activities, not to mention the rules and general environment, are developed for the sole purpose of shaping people into obedient vessels for compliance with State interests and power, by aligning the attitudes and interests of people with those of the State. The State doesn't care whether Piper becomes a "wholesome person" or even "good person." The State cares about maintaining power, and spends energy on its people when they are troublesome and need to be formed into pliant, uncomplicated participants in the system that perpetuates its own authority.

In the book *Orange Is the New Black* that inspired the TV series, the author speaks of prisoners beset by an overwhelming number of written and unwritten rules that new prisoners must learn, and learn fast. Accidentally breaking unknown rules produces punishments ranging from solitary confinement to social ostracism. What prisoners learn deeply is to follow arbitrary and confusing regulations without questioning them, because the consequences for failing to do so might be even more horrendous than their current experience.

What happened to that delicious urge to break the rules, feel the thrill, and return back to safety? Inside prison walls, the eyes of the State are everywhere. Prisoners are subject to numerous counts and inspections, to rooms shared with four or more other women, to sleeping exposed on top of the bed so that it will pass inspection, and, for meeting with someone in the outside world, the ultimate in state surveillance—strip, bend over, and cough, to reveal anything hidden within.

According to this way of looking at prisons, then, *Orange Is the New Black* can be a springboard for considering what is really happening in advanced Western States. And what is happening is homogenization of individuals with State interests; internal states of individuals are being coded and "mapped" by State mechanisms of power. The view of the series from Foucault's ten-thousand-foot vantage point shows us that not only are individuals in prisons forced to internalize acceptance of State power structures and interests, but

all individuals in States must do so as well or face puni-
tive measures.

But what precisely constitutes State power structures and interest? First and foremost, there is obedi-
ence to the law. The law, then, is no longer a primary
principle that agents are supposed to recognize as a good
as part of a social contract, but instead as a mechanism
of State power, purely and simply understood. Piper and
all of the other inmates have not violated a social contract as much as they have broken laws that represent
the raw power of the State to perpetuate itself.

Likewise, people are supposed to willingly participate in the official State economic system, which is cap-
italism. Witness Piper and the other inmates in the
shop. They are being instructed in learning trades, as
well as in how to absorb the rudiments of accepting hierarchical power relations. Inmates who refuse to absorb these lessons over time are going to spend more
time in prison; inmates who learn this lesson, however,
are going to be "productive" members of society upon release, which is to say they're going to be compliant cogs
in the wheel of capitalist productivity, obediently churn-
ing out widgets for other members of society to use in
their equally obedient, capitalist conforming tasks. Also
witness how ordinary commercial items become
grounds for war: women fight over ice cream, trade life-
saving food for jalapeno back lotion, and strangle and
beat one another for access to contraband cosmetics.

Accepting hierarchical power relations is another
way of saying prisoners must be made to be subservient
to authority figures, which is a major part of what the
prison experience is about. In order to ensure their own
safety, Piper and her fellow prisoners must obey the di-
rectives of all prison personnel, from warden to management to psychologist. In turn, when they leave

prison they will be more amenable to playing the kinds of roles expected of compliant citizens.

Finally, one of the mechanisms of State power subtly evidenced in *Orange Is the New Black* is that of the specialist. Prison wardens are specialists in their domain of authority, passing judgment over prisoners on a daily basis in the implicit application of hierarchy. Doctors and psychologists are specialists on the technical-medical model, gaining intimate knowledge of prisoners and their minds so that biographical and psychological knowledge of them serves to transform the abnormal into the normal, the unhealthy into the healthy, all with an eye toward reinforcing State power. And lawyers are probably the most obvious specialists who serve to mold prisoners in relation to State power. Specialization becomes a State strategy for and methodology of securing its own interests.

But notice, *the prisoners also specialize*, and they do it to survive. Anything one prisoner has to offer can bring them power in a world of have-nots. Running the kitchen means access to foodstuffs desired by others, so others must find skills or items to trade. We have a beautician running a salon, a silent and careful listener who can find hidden cigarettes, a yoga teacher and spiritual guide, a van driver with extra soap, street knowledge, and shampoo to offer. Insiders find ways to wiggle into the heart of Healy by supporting his need to feel helpful in group therapy, or trade information with Mr. Caputo to support his need for power and revenge. Of course, Vee simply does what she does—supply drugs to the masses who would like to escape from reality. But everyone has a specialty, and specialization stops us from seeing the surveillance all around us. We look down and focus on the task at hand rather than see the cameras or look toward the stars in awe.

By Hook or by Crook

One of the severest mechanisms by which the State forces through imprisonment the absorption of its "values," or its power, is by removing the access point that prisoners have to their own internal states: privacy. The federal prison in *Orange Is the New Black* is configured in such a way that guards constantly watch what prisoners do; prisoners watch what other prisoners do; walls dividing the living spaces are removed so that guards and other prisoners can view the entire room from end to end, removing any expectation of privacy; mail is read; living spaces are constantly searched. In short, all spaces are surveilled. The prison is a disciplinarian of the State, constricting any hope of psychological freedom and ensuring inmates absorb State mechanisms of power by hook or by crook.

Big Brother

We learn that Piper's brother has subtle insights into her behavior and attitudes, gleaned by incremental observational step by observational step over many years. Thus, a picture of Piper can be put together in stages, with bits of information here and there.

Likewise, the State has mechanisms for putting together pictures of us all; every individual has a portrait drawn by the modern State, and the State maintains a kind of discipline over all of its members in this way. But States don't have to *live* with individuals to gather this information. Advances in technology have made it possible for the State to gather the relevant information on citizens (and non-citizens alike) and crafting a picture from a distance.

Surveillance doesn't even have to be as explicit or overt, as it is in *Orange Is the New Black*. Witness the ubiquitous surveillance of citizens via cell phone communications, electronically tracked book and music orders, video recording cameras on every corner, and mining Facebook and other social media for personal information. Our internal and external states are being monitored and captured, and we are all made to be aware of this. Just like the power of the Panopticon wherein guards don't need to vigilantly, constantly watch from the one-way windows, the State *wants* individuals to know they are being watched, tracked, and recorded; just as it happens in the prison in *Orange Is the New Black*, individuals will begin to police themselves. This in turn assists the State in enforcing its mechanisms of power.

The Full Panopticonic Circle

This brings us around to a reconsideration of our initial query regarding why the series should be so enjoyable, and indeed so popular, yet have as its focus such an unremarkable main character. With Foucault's assistance, we can see the show in a slightly different light, and understand the dilemma as follows: *Orange Is the New Black* very subtly provokes viewers to address these issues, to become aware through episodic exposure that the show itself *embodies* a mechanism of State power. *We are all aware at some level that this is what life in a modern state has become.*

One way or another we are, each of us, prisoner and free citizen and non-citizen alike, made to absorb and adopt the authority of the State and the "values" that the State demands we inhabit. We aren't just looking in at a story about life among people in a women's prison. We are in a sense among the incarcerated, forever under the watchful eye of the State. We no longer have a choice in the matter.

Uncatchable Chickens

Or do we? There is some reason for being hopeful against the doom and gloom that accompanies this interpretation of the function of prisons and State power in general. This hope is to be found, of all places, in persons. Persons can resist systems of power, which luckily have evolved not as deliberate monolithic entities obsessed with their own authority but as accidents that just happen to have evolved into collections and connections of power. Resistance is not futile!

Amy Winehouse in her own way and Rob Ford in his own way refused to absorb and adopt the State-driven values of abstinence and rehabilitation. Indeed, artistic types in general and acts of creativity in particular seem to be a way for persons to get a foothold into exploring their own freedom without complete control of the State overwhelming them, and oftentimes in deliberate opposition to the State. This seems to represent an instance when contrarianism for the sake of contrarianism is a virtue.

Prisons can't control all aspects of individuals' lives and thinking. There are plenty of activities taking place inside the prison walls that reflect the state's inability to control human beings entirely. Likewise, several characters in *Orange Is the New Black* refuse in their own ways to bow to State power, and actively attempt to establish their own sense of identity and authority outside the limits demarcated by the State and its institutions.

Consider Crazy Eyes, the probably mentally unstable inmate whose strange visage is so disturbing that we suspect most viewers hardly give her a second thought after the episodes in which she is "courting" Piper. Unlike Piper, she definitely is someone who fails the Pretty Picture test. Her personality is so bizarre that most viewers will have trouble relating to her. But she clearly has a subtle awareness of her own power and authority against the prison rules and of establishing her own authority. She recites poetry, including Shakespeare, and composes her own poetry.

Recall also the disturbingly draining scene where we viewers are on the edge of our seats wondering what she's going to do in retaliation for Piper's rebuke of her affections, and then the relief, so to speak, of the strange yet provocative act of urinating in the entry to Piper's sleeping quarters. The very act of standing and peeing is deviant, and it is just this element of human behavior, deviance, that might reasonably serve to demarcate individual refusal to absorb and adopt State power and values. There is an unparalleled and necessary element of freedom represented in Crazy Eyes that is evidenced in all persons who do not quite fit in, who aren't part of the acceptable personalities and personae that populate proper society.

The Pied Piper Revisited

The Pied Piper is a story of a man who is hired to lead the rats out of the village with his unique, individual powers. He accomplishes the task, and the town, en masse, refuses to pay him—a power play. The Piper stands up to the State, and using his unique individual powers, leads their children away just like he led the rats away. He takes their future, and causes the whole town to stand still in time.

Piper Chapman is on the other side of the town boundary—standing still in time herself. She was just one of the townspeople, happily willing to ignore whether or not there is justice for all, as long as she is among the privileged. She re-joins the powerful white upper middle class after her adventures into marginal society. She plays out a sort of fantasy for all of us who are sitting watching TV; we don't know a single person who has not, at some point, broken the law. But we do know that if we have a certain status in society, we can get away with a few things here and there. And Piper, ten years after her crimes, seems to be a productive member of society, selling handmade scented bath soap and toiletries to upscale merchants with exclusive clientele.

She does draw us, the average viewer, in, because we feel for her—for Piper, consequences came, and for us, they didn't. Her character seduces us with the message that she didn't really deserve to go to prison because she isn't really a criminal like the other characters— she just had a little adventure post-college, but she doesn't belong there. . . . she's like us. So we think.

Until we meet the other characters. Really meet them. We go inside and get turned out. The other characters represent the margins of society—the foreigners, the mentally ill, the transgender—each with special powers that central society enjoys but refuses to pay for. They clean our houses, comprise our churches, and serve as boundaries for us as the normal and them as the figures who provide entertainment in drag shows or figures we pity and care for, showing how good we are. What's revealed in the show is that Piper doesn't have stand-up values. She wants to hide under the guise of normalcy. But those who are marginalized outside are accustomed to working for every bit of power that a power-hungry State denies them.

They know how to fight. Red would kidnap your children, Vee may well go further. Don't those women have any values? Aren't they out of control? But we are confronted with Piper as someone who also trades on her values, who runs back and forth between Larry and Alex wildly looking for who can provide more emotional comfort, security, and stability as she is cast outside the town walls and inside prison walls. And the lines blur. Who doesn't have any values? Who is bad?

The show is a confrontation of the fact that those who participate in the expectations of the State are not better, just safer. And we slowly begin to identify with Red, with Nicky, with Poussey, these outsiders who have kept their values in spite of State power relationships that oppress them. Despite its reflection of the sometimes overwhelming power of the State, *Orange Is the New Black* also sends a message about a kind of subversive, unbreakable element of the human spirit. And that's a tune we'll happily follow to the series finale!

8
Who's Messing with Your Mind?

MYISHA CHERRY

"She just ran game on you." "You got played!" "He plays mind games." "You were brainwashed!" What's the meaning of these statements? They all express the realization that you've been a victim of manipulation.

I remember the first time I heard the term "manipulation." I was a pre-teen and one of my adult mentors was warning me about a close friend of mine who they believed was a manipulator. They felt she had played them and was playing me too.

"Manipulation" was a big word for me at the time and although I didn't know what it meant, I knew it meant something bad. As I grew older, I thought I'd finally understood the meaning of the term. I was experiencing life, horrible people, and retained something from my psychology 101 course. I had also read my share of Dale Carnegie and Robert Greene books. But all of my previous experiences could not compare to the crash course in manipulation I received while watching Season Two of *Orange Is the New Black*.

I'm not a psychologist. I'm a philosopher interested in moral psychology. While psychologists analyze behavior, I am interested in the nature and moral status of attitudes, dispositions, and emotions such as compassion, anger, forgiveness, and manipulation. But it's one thing to sit in an armchair and philosophize about these ideas and it's another thing altogether to see an idea embodied in a character. Yvonne "Vee" Parker is that character.

Vee makes her *Orange Is the New Black* debut in Season Two ("Looks Blue, Tastes Red") in the backstory of Tasha "Taystee" Jefferson's life. As a child, Taystee is a ward of the state who desires to get adopted. Vee is a drug dealer in Taystee's community who tries to recruit her as a child and throughout her teenage years. Taystee refuses her offer until foster care life begins to get the best of her.

With tears running down her face, Taystee begs Vee to take her in. She then shows Vee her skill with numbers when a desperate customer who defaulted on his payments comes in to re-up on drugs. Vee is persuaded and decides to take her into her home. Vee also employees Taystee in her drug business. In the flashback scenes, it appears as if Vee is giving Taystee everything she has been yearning for: stability, support, home-cooked meals, and a family.

While watching, I started to feel happy for Taystee and also confused. I didn't know what Vee's intentions were. Was she sincere and loving or was she taking care of Taystee for all the wrong reasons? It's not until Vee begins to do time at Litchfield Penitentiary that I see that she is a master manipulator who repeatedly 'runs game' on everyone.

What Is Manipulation?

You are a pedophile without the sex. I bet the real playas laugh in your face.

—POUSSEY ("Take a Break from Your Values")

Philosophers are divided on what manipulation is. This isn't because manipulation is hard to define; it's because manipulation has so many features and these features do not always fit all cases of manipulation. One definition is that manipulation is covert influence over another. The person who's being manipulated doesn't know what's actually happening. To manipulate, you must keep your true intentions hidden. Vee's victims are completely oblivious in the moment to what she is up to and are usually enraged when they find out. Her actions fit this definition.

Other philosophers define manipulation as non-rational influence of some sort. Instead of laying out a logical argument where she says that Pousey needs to be shut off from the group because she turns down opportunities to make money, Vee instead convinces Taystee through homophobia, to stay away from Pousey. She persuades Taystee through non-rational influence. In this way, Vee is the sophist of her day. The sophists were Socrates's nemeses in Ancient Greece. While Socrates argued by and for rational persuasion, the sophists used emotions, rhetorical tricks, and manipulation to persuade their audience. Vee neglects rational influence and opts for persuasion of a psychological kind instead.

Some definitions of manipulation tend to focus on the effect of the non-rational influence. Manipulation then can be described as behavior that makes the listener make decisions in ways that rational people wouldn't want to make decisions. When Mendoza realizes they are smoking cigarettes that are from 1983, she screams out, "that bitch!" because she knows that if she had only known they were that old, she would not had made the cake-cigarette deal with Vee. The effect of Vee's non-rational influence is that it causes

Mendoza to make decisions she would not normally rationally make, but while under the influence of manipulation in this case, she does. As you can see, Vee's actions satisfy this definition of manipulation as well.

Manipulation's Ammo Is Emo

Manipulation also has several features. In order for manipulation to take place, Colin McGinn argues in his book *MindFucking: A Critique of Mental Manipulation*, that trust, deception, emotion, false belief, and vulnerability must be present. The manipulator gets the listener to trust them and deceives them in the process by implanting false beliefs. For McGinn, the most important of these features are emotions. Manipulation aims to make you think something that is not true but also to *feel* a certain way. Manipulation produces false belief but it also produces emotional disturbance. The manipulator has to play on your emotions in order to create the false belief.

This takes skill. In the instances of Vee's manipulation trek, she uses emotions brilliantly. She plays into Taystee's fear of being perceived as gay, Poussey's desire to be loved, Mendoza's sympathy, and Crazy Eyes's desire to be seen, valued, and accepted. Vee uses these emotions as a starting point in order to create the false belief that it's best for Taystee to stay away from Poussey, Poussey to stay away from Taystee, Mendoza to request that her girls join custodial, and Crazy Eyes to be loyal to Vee.

To use emotions effectively, the manipulator must be a psychologist who is a student of human weakness and vulnerability. Anne Barnhill has given an account of manipulation in terms of targeting weaknesses. For Barnhill, manipulation is intentionally making someone or altering a situation to make someone succumb to a weakness or a contextual weakness. Vee is an evil Dr. Phil, scoping out the details of people's personalities and histories to discover their weakness and then using that weakness against them. She sits in the meeting where Nicky testifies to the fact that although she's been clean for two years, heroin is her best friend and she misses the way it makes her feel. Days later, Vee sends her a bag of heroin through a dealer with the message, "First one's free, let me know if you want more." Here Vee alters a situation to get Nicky to succumb to her weakness so that Vee can profit.

In the same episode, Vee also mysteriously sees the weakness of Black Cindy. After Cindy comes up short and then challenges her, Vee visits her bunk with a psychological analysis. Vee 'reads' Cindy by telling her that Cindy is all about jokes, she has given up on herself, and is a loser. In this episode we see the backstory to Cindy's life. On the outside she was always joking, didn't take life too seriously, didn't have the means to take care of her daughter or the courage to let her daughter know she was her mom. This tormented her. The audience sees Cindy's life but Vee doesn't. However, Vee is still able to know Cindy's weakness. Through this conversation, Vee makes Cindy succumb to her weakness of wanting to prove herself. It will lead Cindy to come back to Vee to deal drugs.

Some philosophers even argue that because the manipulator trades on the vulnerabilities of the victim, the victim is complicit in their own victimization. This is in no way blaming the victim but it is to suggest that the manipulator is only successful because they exploit only what's already present in the victim. If the victim were not gullible, the manipulator couldn't appeal to their gullible tendency. If the victim were not sympathetic, the manipulator couldn't appeal to their sympathetic tendency. There are people that Vee does not manipulate and it makes us wonder that perhaps it's because of their emotional strengths or their lack of *visible* vulnerabilities that keep them safe from her snares.

Although McGinn highlights the importance of emotions in manipulation, Robert Noggle believes that there are three main ways that you can manipulate someone and they are through belief, desire, and emotion. He gives no significance to one over the other. He calls these 'levelers' and the person you are manipulating, a machine. For Noggle, manipulation takes place by leading someone away from the ideal version of his or her belief, desire, and emotion.

For example, an ideal desire could be to stay out of trouble and out of the dramas of prison life. Anne Barnhill modifies Noggle's definition by suggesting that the manipulator must be aware that there is a steering away of the listener from their ideal place. When Vee manipulates Mendoza by suggesting that she gives up the bathroom in return for Taystee and Watson joining the custodial crew, it is Red who has to make Mendoza aware of what she has really done and how Vee has 'played' her. The custodial crew will be responsible for the drug trade in the prison. Vee led Mendoza away from her ideal desire of not contributing to trouble and Vee was very much aware that it was far away from Mendoza's ideal desire.

Although the manipulator implants false beliefs, this is not to say that manipulators do not *express* the truth. The manipulator doesn't always speak something false. Manipulators can be misleading without speaking falsely. As Jason Stanley has pointed out, you can state a truth and rely on the listener's false belief to communicate your goals. When Vee tells Poussey that Taystee will never love her the way she wants, Vee is not speaking falsely. Taystee communicated something similar to Poussey earlier. However, Vee is misleading Poussey into accepting the false belief that Taystee does not care about her and is not really her friend.

Manipulation is also tricky (no pun intended). It can include emotions, but not always. It can be contrary to the victim's interests, but can be in their best interests. It can aim at changing someone's behavior or changing a decision. It can play on someone's personality but also widely shared dispositions. Vee uses cake in "A Whole 'Nother Hole" to reconcile with Taystee and to get the others to warm up to her. Even for her to get the cake, she uses old cigarettes to seduce Mendoza into giving her the food. Although she has not manipulated them through their emotions or weaknesses this time, she knows the psychological power that baked goods and a good cigarette has to unite troops and also make deals.

As we can see, manipulation can take many different forms. Vee's manipulative actions seem to cover all of them-proving that she is not only a skillful psychologist, but a multi-talented one as well.

What's Wrong with Manipulation?

She is a truth teller. Don't you dare speak ill of her!

—CRAZY EYES ("We Have Manners. We're Polite")

There must be something morally problematic with manipulation that will make Vee's manipulative actions unethical. Under what conditions can we say that manipulation is bad?

Before we try to get at what's bad about Vee's actions and character (that's the easy part), let's try to imagine Vee's manipulation as a good thing. What would make her manipulative actions good? Aristotle might argue that to be a manipulator you must know how to bring about conduct at the right time, for the right reason, and to accomplish the right ends. It appears as if Vee has this skill down perfectly. She gets her girls in custodial at the right time (she "bargained" at a perfect time to make it happen), for the right reason (to obtain advantages), and for the right ends (nicotine relaxation for inmates).

This is skillful maneuvering. This would qualify her actions as virtuous, right? Let's not go too far. Skillful acts do not equate to ethical acts. Serial killers and Wall Street criminals can use skillful methods and perfect application of those methods in their criminal activities but that is not enough to then evaluate their actions as ethical.

In addition, Vee's case is not like a friend who manipulates their drunken friend to turn over their keys or their sick friend to finally visit the doctor. In these cases, a friend can be accused of manipulation, particularly if they use non-rational or covert influence, but we would not judge their actions to be unethical. The reason is because although they too are using strategic application of Aristotle's advice, they are aiming for a good result on behalf of the listener, and their manipulative actions are coupled with concern, compassion and sympathy. Vee is only thinking of herself. We can say that Vee has a skill to do manipulative actions in a skillful way, but this skill should not be interpreted as virtuous or ethical. Her actions will have to be more than skillful to be considered morally good.

Vee's manipulative actions toward her fellow inmates are morally problematic because her manipulation threatens her listener's autonomy, she employs certain vices, and bad consequences arise as a result.

Most criticisms of manipulation focus on its threat to the autonomy of the listener. When someone manipulates you, you're kept in the dark and as a result you're less free in your decision-making. But threats to autonomy involve more than this. When Vee manipulates, she imposes her will on her listeners in ways that they would not endorse if they knew what was going on. Melvin Rogers has argued that when we manipulate, we dominate the listener by substituting our judgment and will for the listener's own, and secure their co-operation to our advantage. He argues that this violates what Rogers calls the *identifiability condition* because the listener no longer recognizes himself or herself in the belief they now hold.

Vee also blocks and burdens her listeners' options. Instead of giving Taystee a choice in helping her with a new jail hustle, Vee manipulates her by holding what she did for her as a child, over her head. Taystee feels like she has no other options because of this demand and obligation for loyalty. Although Taystee is aware of what has taken place, her autonomy is still threatened. Vee is imposing her will over Taystee in ways that Taystee would not endorse otherwise. She thus becomes Vee's slave, lacking full autonomy. Persons ought not to be used in this way. In a Kantian sense, the glory of our being is in our rationality. To have that under the submission of another is to deny us our personhood and that is what Vee does when she manipulates.

Manipulation also employs many vices and these vices make Vee's actions bad. According to J.S. Blumenthal-Barby, to manipulate you must employ dishonesty, predatoriness, disrespect, and laziness. Vee is dishonest when she tells Red that the war between them is over. Vee is a predator by not only exploiting the weaknesses of her fellow inmates but by making Taystee feel indebted to her. She tells her "You owe me."

Vee disrespects her fellow inmates by not seeing them as persons but rather as pawns and objects that can be used for her own purposes. Look at how she nonverbally instructs Crazy Eyes to beat up Poussey in the bathroom. Vee is also lazy. She does not try to convince anyone through rational arguments but takes the easy way out through psychological persuasion.

In addition, Vee's manipulative actions do not aim for the good. Okay, they aim for *her own* good, but they do not aim for the good of those who are the targets of her manipulation. It's her dealers who possess the illegal contraband not her, increasing the risk that it's they who will get caught. When the correctional officers do a sweep of the prison, Janae is caught and taken to the SHU, not Vee.

Her victims usually suffer bad consequences. When Vee assaults Red, she convinces Crazy Eyes that it was Crazy Eyes that did it for her. Vee wanted Crazy Eyes to take the rap, knowing that the consequence for the assault would be an attempted murder charge and movement to maximum security. Niccolò Machiavelli, the sixteenth-century Italian political theorist, wrote that "Although the act condemns the doer, the end may justify him." Vee is Machiavellian in this way. Vee thinks that immoral means justify her aim for survival and glory.

Protect Yourself

Don't feel bad if you don't see it yet. . . . I just hope y'all wise up before it's too late.

—TAYSTEE ("We Have Manners. We're Polite")

I think I've discovered ways for manipulators like Vee to be stopped in their tracks, ways that don't include shanking them or doing a literal 'drive by' in a van. What you are about to read is not a Sun Tzu "Art of War" discourse. This is not to downplay philosophy, but we are no experts of war. However, I think philosophy can give us some insights into how to guard ourselves against manipulators.

You don't have to be an expert in manipulation either. You just have to learn a few critical thinking skills and tips from philosophers like Socrates and Immanuel Kant and soon you'll be able to protect yourself from the Vees of the world.

The first thing we can do is to improve our critical thinking skills. This involves being able to recognize and evaluate arguments. The only arguments we ought to accept are those resulting in conclusions backed by true premises that are appropriately related to one another. We should guard against being seduced by appeals to our emotions, popularity, tradition, irrelevant information, and more. This will take psychological strength because humans have psychological needs and manipulation feeds off of this. But if former drug addict, Nicky, can give over to Red the free bag of heroin that was given to her, we can refuse the psychological drugs manipulators peddle to us.

Immanuel Kant argues that emotions should have no room in ethical reasoning. For Kant, emotions come and go, so we ought not to depend on them to make decisions. Emotions can cloud our judgments because they can force us to give excessive credulity in judgment. They also can make us less prone to revise our judgments in light of reflection. I'm not arguing that emotions have no cognitive features or any room in persuasion or ethics, rather I'm suggesting that being convinced through emotions alone and not by true and strong propositions will make us susceptible to manipulators.

Socrates agrees. For him, rhetoricians like his Gorgias (in Plato's dialogue *Gorgias*), use emotional appeals, particularly flattery, to convince the masses. Because of this, Socrates claims that those who listen to Gorgias are witnessing an *experience* but not an *art*. Reasoning is not what Gorgias does. Those who give into a modern day Gorgias are not reasoning either. Because manipulation plays on the emotions in order to implant false beliefs, we should be careful to make sure that it's rationality and not emotion that leads us to accept the conclusions of arguments. If not, we will be suckered every time.

Lastly, Socrates says in *The Apology* that the unexamined life is not worth living. Careful examination should be a part of our internal lives and our engagement with others. This is not to say that we ought to be skeptics each time someone attempts to persuade us of something but it does suggest that we ought to hold others to high standards when it comes to convincing us of anything. We should not believe everything we hear but ought to inspect everything for its truth and give ourselves time to do so. Unscrupulous operators will continue to play us if we fail to stop and think, truth-check, and evaluate the motive behind people's attempts to persuade.

V

To eat the chicken that chicken that is smarter than other chickens

9
Take a Break from Your Values

RACHEL ROBISON-GREENE

In "Hugs Can Be Deceiving," a group of prisoners is on a hunger strike to try to get better living conditions in the prison. Leanne and Angie (who, in the outside world weren't too successful with monitoring their intake of substances to begin with) are tempted to break their strike by eating some of the Little Caesar's pizza that the guards wave under their noses.

One of them grabs a slice. When the others protest she exclaims, "I'm just licking it!" (Of course that doesn't count.) Sister Ingalls says to the tempted, "Go ahead girls. Take a break from your values." She comforts Soso, insisting that their movement is no worse off, as Leanne and Angie are weak.

Prison conditions are rough. In some ways they're supposed to be. Is prison a place where we can and perhaps even should "take a break from your values"? Can we manage to be morally good in a place like Litchfield?

The Ideal Meets the Real

All problems are boring until they're your own.

—RED ("Low Self Esteem City")

Some people believe that the basic principles of morals apply to an ideal world. In real life, things get too messy to simply apply the basic principles.

One philosopher who thinks like this is John Rawls, in his classic work, *A Theory of Justice*. Rawls splits morality—in this case the morality of justice—into two parts. There is an "ideal" part where we try to imagine a system of perfect justice, then there's the "non-ideal" part where we try to apply that system to what Rawls calls "less happy conditions," which means real life!

Consider someone like Gloria Mendoza, the new Latina head of the kitchen at Litchfield. Mendoza was incarcerated for food stamp fraud. Her crime, like most, wasn't victimless, but her motivation for committing the crime was to get herself and her son out of an abusive relationship with a very violent man. What do we want to say about her crime? My reaction to the revelation of Mendoza's backstory (presented in the Season Two episode, "Low Self Esteem City") was sympathetic. Should she really be serving time in prison for committing that particular crime for that particular reason?

Idealizations may serve to further the interests of the group that already has the power because, often, the people who construct idealized theories are themselves members of the powerful class. It might be easy, then, to overlook the experiences and interests of less advantaged groups in coming up with a moral theory. Contrast someone like Mendoza with someone like Larry. Larry is (inexplicably given that he writes for a living) a middle class, young, white man. When we make an idealized moral pronouncement to Larry, it isn't going to be that difficult for him to follow it. When we tell him that it's wrong to steal, he can easily just refrain from stealing. One objection to Ideal Theory is that facts matter. The particular lived experiences of less advantaged groups matter to the development of moral and political systems.

Do you remember Jimmy, the elderly prisoner with a major story arc in Season Two? You might not. As the writers of the show effectively illustrate, the elderly can be invisible in society, especially in a place like prison, and so they're easy to forget. As Frieda points out, "No one gives a shit about old ladies. We remind everyone that they're gonna die."

Jimmy has advanced dementia and escapes from Litchfield. She wanders to a bar where she sits down to listen to music. She is easily recaptured and sent back to prison. A compassionate release is arranged for her. In an ideal world, compassionate releases might be the way they sound—compassionate. However, when we look at the particular facts of Jimmy's experience, we realize that her particulars are very important. Jimmy's health condition is one that renders her incapable of caring for herself, and she has no one on the outside to help her. "Compassionate release" for Jimmy is effectively a new sentence—a death sentence, but one that will be carried out in the streets instead of inside the walls of Litchfield.

Consider also the case of Sophia, a transgender woman who finds herself behind the walls of Litchfield for credit card fraud. She commits the crime in order to pay for gender reassignment surgery (GRS). Credit card fraud isn't pretty. It causes a lot of anxiety for all of the parties involved. Again, however, Sophia's experience and the background conditions that give rise to the circumstances that she finds herself in are relevant to our assessment of the situation as well. Both in the real world and in the *Orange Is the New Black* universe the health needs of transgender individuals are not taken seriously enough. The crime Sophia commits has everything to do with the fact that GRS is not covered by medical insurance. The administrators at Litchfield also somehow think it's appropriate to sacrifice Sophia's hormone pills to "budget cuts," while continuing to provide estrogen pills to Sister Ingalls. The experience of transgender individuals should be taken into account when we construct social policy. Theories that are constructed from the position of some idealized observer, outside the experiences of the people directly involved, may not be up to the task of providing the right kind of moral guidance in these cases.

Irrelevant Ideals

You're one Cheerio in the bulk box of life.

—NICKY ("Thirsty Bird")

Some pretty shady stuff happens at Litchfield. Some of the behavior that takes place at the prison is just pretty clearly immoral—for example, pretty much everything Pornstache ever does. Other kinds of behavior are up for debate. A person has to adapt to survive in prison. This is basically the theme of Season One. By the second episode of the show, Red is already trying to starve Piper out of existence. Circumstances inside the prison are far from the ideal conditions that Rawls has in mind for his theory of justice.

In an environment like this, what happens to morality? Should a person strive to do what they ideally ought to do? Is Piper obligated to always keep her head above the fray and do what an idealized moral theory would tell her to do? Or do the rules of the game change given facts about the situation?

Some of the characters try to maintain a commitment to an idealized system of morality. Take Brook

Soso, who participated in an illegal political protest on the outside and ends up in Litchfield. She is extremely idealistic. When she attempts to bring that idealistic attitude into the prison, she's not taken seriously. She decides to protest the living conditions by starting a hunger strike. She gets Leann, and Angie (newly liberated from the sway of Pennsatucky) to joint the strike with her. She's joined by Yoga Jones, and then, eventually, by Sister Ingalls.

Some of their demands are silly. LeAnn and Angie can't agree whether the prison needs real maple syrup or the imitation stuff, but clearly one kind of syrup constitutes a serious injustice. The same goes for the quality of the laundry detergent. There are more significant issues that the more grounded members of the group want to change. At the beginning of Season Two, there's a plumbing issue in the B Block bathroom that results in waste bubbling up through the drain in the showers. Prisoners are told that the best response to this situation is to wear shoes in the bathroom. Seems a little inhumane. Solitary confinement, what the prisoners call "SHU" is used excessively and often. These issues seem worthy of protest.

Food is an important commodity at Litchfield. Factions gain control over it and use it as a tool both politically and personally. In light of that fact, engaging in a hunger strike is a risky proposition. Red punishes Piper by withholding food, Pornstache gets back at Red by peeing in the Thanksgiving gravy, and the Latinas put too much salt in the food of Vee's gang (but remember the advice Crazy Eyes gives us, "The secret is pretend the salt is sugar.") The practice of keeping individually packaged food bought at commissary is common among the prisoners there. Bottom line: in Litchfield if you have access to food, be grateful. Food isn't a sure thing.

The food-related facts don't matter much to Sosa or to Yoga Jones. They see respect for basic human dignity as something that should be afforded to every individual, incarcerated or not. They have an ideal picture of moral obligation, and they take it to be binding on everyone else as well. Unfortunately, neither the other prisoners nor the guards or administration have much patience for their idealism. They're only able to recruit, in the end, five people to participate in the hunger strike. The administration is not even moderately moved to action by the behavior of the group. After hearing about their demands, Caputo approaches the group:

CAPUTO: You say you want the B dorm bathroom fixed. Done.

GROUP: Yay! We did it!

CAPUTO: You didn't do anything, it was already happening. Now you say you want restrictions on the use of the SHU. What does that mean exactly?

YOGA JONES: There's no accountability. People get thrown in for no reason, for any period of time. Arbitrarily. Watson's been in there like, every other month.

CAPUTO: She brought that on herself. As far as the duration of the stay, there is a system in place with strict guidelines and we are under no obligation to explain to you how it works. But, as it so happens, your friend Watson is coming out today.

GROUP: Yay! Congratulations, Yoga.

CAPUTO: Again, just a coincidence. Nothing to do with this.

Caputo makes it clear that the changes in the prison are happening, but they aren't happening because the administration is impressed with the idealism and activist nature of the inmates. The changes were happening anyway, as it turns out, for reasons that had nothing to do with morality or respect for basic human dignity.

One of the main motivations that Yoga Jones had to join the hunger strike is that she cared about her friend Watson, who was facing SHU more often than many other prisoners for reasons that didn't seem to have much to do with the severity of her infractions. When she talks to Watson after she is released, however, Watson doesn't seem very interested in Yoga's moral concern for her situation. Watson tells Yoga, "I don't really feel like being your token black friend right now."

The idealized perspective of morality is falling on deaf ears at Litchfield. This is far from the only time. Other attempts to do what's right are met with similar degrees of success. Consider, for example, when Sophia runs for WAC, claiming that she wants to improve treatment of the basic human rights of the prisoners. She is asked: "What do you think this is, white people politics?" Taystee is ultimately elected to WAC instead of Sophia.

Piper is also elected to WAC and approaches it as if it could actually be a vehicle she could use to bring about positive social change in the prison. She soon learns that it is simply an opportunity for the administration to make it look as if they care about the input of the prisoners. In practice, they don't care much what the women have to say and Healy tries to buy them off with donuts and coffee at the meetings, leaving Piper to conclude: "His whole WAC thing is basically bullshit" ("Blood Donut").

Ideal theories simply seem to be irrelevant in a place like Litchfield. Rawls suggests that the proper order of theorizing should first be at the level of the ideal and the, once that idealized theory is in place, we can look at the facts about what the world actually looks like and fix the injustices with our ideal theory in mind. There may, however, be places where the ideal theory has very little to say. The ideal theory may be totally irrelevant in those places. Litchfield might be one of those places.

The Facts of Life Inside

The thing about reality is it's still there waiting for you the next morning.

—Rosa ("40 OZ of Furlough")

What else is there if we abandon ideal theory? One approach that we could take is say, "Look, this is prison. My only obligation is to keep myself alive and safe. The time in prison constitutes, for me, a moral holiday. My obligations under these conditions are purely pragmatic. I really can take a break from my values."

But it sounds strange to say that there are certain locations in the world where morality just doesn't work. We don't need to throw out the baby with the bath water. Instead, we should try to work out a morality that isn't based on an ideal world, but starts from the particular situation facing the Litchfield prisoners. So what are some of the features of life inside Litchfield that make it less than ideal?

One obvious and unfortunate feature of prison is that races self-segregate. In the outside world, many people genuinely value ethnic diversity in their lives. Many others at least pay lip service to the idea of diversity, even if they don't try to promote diversity in their own lives. In Litchfield, ethnic groups keep to themselves and power structures are created within those groups. When the B Block bathroom is flooded, the response is not to just go ahead and desegregate the bathrooms, but to play politics between the racial groups on the topic of who gets which bathroom.

There's obviously discrimination coming both from the administration and from the other prisoners on the basis of gender identity and sexual orientation as well. We've seen the discrimination that Sophia deals with when it comes to getting the health care she needs, but in addition to oppression on that level, she also faces discrimination from other inmates because of her gender identity.

Orange Is the New Black, jam-packed as it is with lesbian sex, also portrays characters being discriminated against on the basis of sexual orientation. When Healy finds out that Piper and Alex used to be involved on a sexual level, he starts treating Piper, formerly a favorite of his, much differently. When he finds out that Piper is again involved with Alex, he throws her in the SHU, which is traumatizing for the inmates that have to experience it. Lesbian characters also have much to fear from other inmates. People like Pennsatucky (at least the Pennsatucky we meet in Season One) hate homosexuals of any sort and want to hurt them (recall that Pennsatucky locked Alex in a dryer).

Prisoners have good reason to be afraid of violence in Litchfield. They have very good reason to be concerned that their personal property (to the extent that they really have any) will be taken away either by other inmates or by the staff of the prison. Litchfield prisoners are also afraid of more serious threats of violence. They fear rape and unwanted sexual attention, not only from other prisoners, but also from the staff. Pornstache establishes himself as a proper target of this fear early in the series. Prisoners, in many cases, are justified in feeling fear for their physical health and even for their very lives. We've seen some pretty tough cookies in Litchfield, and many of them are willing to injure and kill, even inside the walls.

Moreover, inmates are put in a position in which as we've seen, their voices are not heard. They don't have an opportunity to participate in any sort of political process. This is to be expected: they're in prison, after all. They are being punished for bad things that they've done. All the same, when we make social policy or construct a system of morality, the facts that are true of people having these experiences might be relevant to the assessment of what we should be doing.

Right and Wrong in Relationships

I know something about loving people who aren't smart enough to love back.

—CRAZY EYES ("You Also Have a Pizza")

Care Ethics is an ethical theory that is attractive to many thinkers whose sympathies lie with ideal theory rather than non-ideal theory. It is attractive because it is appropriately sensitive to the facts of experience. This form of ethics is, in many ways distinct from other kinds of ethical theories. Instead of focusing on particular acts, care ethics is concerned with relationships. In prison or outside of it, we find ourselves in relationships with other people. People sometimes find themselves cast in the role of the provider of care. In other circumstances, they find themselves in the role of the care recipient. Both parties in the relationship have responsibilities—they both have role-based duties.

Take, for example, the relationship that exists between a parent and a child. The parent obviously has certain important obligations to the child. The parent needs to teach the child how to be a responsible adult, to educate the child, and to be a good example to the child. The parent has an obligation to keep the child safe from harm. The child also has duties to the parent. The child has the obligation to try to understand what's being taught, to listen to the parent's advice about safety, and to try to follow that advice. They both have an obligation to demonstrate love toward one another.

We find ourselves cast in many roles that come with many relationship-based obligations. Those obligations will be different depending on the kind of relationship we enter into. Crucially though, to satisfy the obligations that our roles give rise to, we need to be sensitive to the facts of the case.

If I'm a parent, I need to see to it that my child is safe, but that might mean very different things from one child to the next. If my child has a disability of some sort, that might dramatically change what I am obligated to do for him. If my child is an advanced learner, that might change my obligations with regard to his education.

This is a moral theory that can find a home in Litchfield. We can understand the relationships between the various factions in this way. A person can form relationships or they can remain alienated like Miss Claudette. To the extent that they enter into relationships, they take on moral responsibilities of care. The exact nature of those obligations will be sensitive to the particular facts of the case.

Morals on the Outside

It's a metaphor, you potato with eyes!

—PENNSATUCKY ("You Also Have a Pizza")

We've looked at how ideal and non-ideal theory work, or don't work, inside Litchfield. Ideal Theory may actually be best in an environment in which Rawls's main assumptions are true—people find themselves in roughly equally circumstances and are generally willing to follow the kinds of rules that an ideal theory of justice would prescribe. People in Litchfield (almost by stipulation, given that they are in prison) are not willing to follow the rules. But perhaps Ideal Theory really does make more sense in the outside world.

Or maybe not. Some of the people in Litchfield are real social deviants, but many of them are not. Many (perhaps most) of them are average people of the type that you might meet on any day of the week outside of prison. The world comprises these kinds of people.

People make mistakes. Some of those mistakes are also violations of law. Some of them aren't. The basic social dynamics that exist inside the prison also exist outside of prison. The prison system may be a particularly powerful metaphor, but it may be more than a metaphor. It may also constitute a microcosm of society in general. There are rule followers and there are rule breakers, and some who generally follow rules but are willing to make some exceptions. People belong to different cultural communities, face different challenges, and have different conceptions of justice. People experience oppression outside the prison—oppression that might not be fully comprehended by people who are not oppressed in just that way.

So, if a non-ideal theory of ethics makes most sense in a place like Litchfield, it might also make most sense in the wider world outside. I'll leave that to you to decide.

10
You're Not Religious, Okay

Seth M. Walker

Okay. So, what? Well, apparently Piper's irreligious beliefs resulted in her making a joke out of Pennsatucky's supposed "faith healing" abilities, "almost ruining" her life in the process. That's what—and that's an understandable reason to hold a grudge and demand an apology (though awkwardly disguised as asking for forgiveness from God). But, even though the clash between Tiffany "Pennsatucky" Doggett and Piper Chapman started long before this exchange in the first season, this episode ("Fool Me Once") marked a very important moment in the series: we discover Piper's personal beliefs about the world and how they differ from the beliefs of people like Pennsatucky.

Pennsatucky's theistic worldview, specifically a form of right-wing Christian fundamentalism, contrasts the secular humanism Piper confesses to during that same exchange. And Pennsatucky's remarks imply that Piper's worldview is worth less than the one Pennsatucky embraces (but let's not forget, she's still pretty upset about the faith healing incident):

PENNSATUCKY: What do you believe in?

123

PIPER: Well, I've always thought that "agnostic" was sort of a cop-out. But, um, you know if I had to label it, I'd say that I'm a secular humanist, which is not to say I'm not spiritual—

PENNSATUCKY: —You're not religious, okay. Just stop. Stop.

When you're stuck in a cell for anywhere between fourteen months (such as Piper) to the end of your life (such as Rosa Cisneros, though her exact place of departure remains to be seen), the only way to maintain some sort of sanity is by making your experience as meaningful as possible. "It's all temporary," Erica "Yoga" Jones tells Piper in the first episode ("I Wasn't Ready"), and the way to survive in prison is "to make something as meaningful and beautiful as you can" out of your experience there.

For Pennsatucky, we know her Christian faith is supposedly doing the trick—allowing her to do her time and "make something out of it." But, what about Piper? The way Pennsatucky confronts her and passively belittles her beliefs suggests that she doesn't believe Piper *can* have a meaningful existence if she's at odds with her and not "right with Him." Whether we agree with Pennsatucky's views or not, we get the gist of what she believes and how that directs her life. But, again, what about Piper? What does it mean that she's a secular humanist, and how can she make a meaningful existence for herself in light of this perspective—both inside the prison and out—without the saving grace and moral guidance of an all-powerful deity?

I'd Say that I'm a Secular Humanist

Later on in "Fool Me Once," right after Piper opts out of being dunked for a muck sink-baptism, she takes the opportunity to elaborate on what she started saying earlier:

> I can't pretend to believe in something I don't. And I don't
> . . . I believe in science. I believe in evolution. . . . I cannot get
> behind some supreme being who weighs in on the Tony
> Awards while a million people get whacked with machetes. I
> don't believe a billion Indians are going to hell. I don't think
> we get cancer to learn life lessons, and I don't believe that
> people die young because God needs another angel. I think
> it's just bullshit, and on some level I think we all know that. I
> mean, don't you? . . . Look, I understand that religion makes
> it easier to deal with all of the random shitty things that hap-
> pen to us. And I wish I could get on that ride. I'm sure I would
> be happier. But, I can't. Feelings aren't enough. I need it to
> be real.

This powerful rant places Piper and Pennsatucky at odds once again, but also highlights some of the key aspects and aims of secular humanism. Let's take a closer look at Piper's views and see how they relate to the meaning she's trying to find.

I Believe in Science. I Believe in Evolution

Paul Kurtz, one of the key figures in the development of contemporary secular humanism, sums up the philosophical position as one that "rejects supernatural accounts of reality" but "seeks to optimize the fullness of human life in a naturalistic universe." According to Kurtz in *What Is Secular Humanism?* the "secular humanist paradigm" has six key features:

1. **It is a method of inquiry**

2. **It provides a naturalistic cosmic outlook**

3. **It is nontheistic**

4. **It is committed to humanistic ethics**

5. **It offers a democratic perspective**

6. **It is planetary in scope**

The first two characteristics echo Piper's belief in science and evolution, and the third is clear throughout the remainder of her rant. The fifth and sixth are broader objectives and goals within the movement, reflecting a concern with equality and justice and the fact that nations can no longer solve their varying problems alone—especially when those problems affect the planet at a much wider scale and depend on other nations to resolve. But, what about that fourth characteristic: being committed to humanistic ethics? We're going to see that the secular humanist perspective can involve quite a shift in our understanding of what is "good" and how we can live a meaningful life.

Since secular humanists aren't theistic, they obviously aren't getting their ethical values and moral guidance from any sort of supernatural deity or metaphysical realm. The emphasis is on human freedom and responsibility: Piper is in control of her own life, shaping her own future (Goodbye, Larry!) and destiny, making of herself what she wills. In this way, the humanist outlook overlaps quite a bit with twentieth-century existential philosophy, which can help us better understand what is needed for her to live a meaningful life.

Make Something Out of It

Jean-Paul Sartre (1905–1980) famously indicated that existentialism *is* a humanism in his 1945 lecture of the same name ("Existentialism Is a Humanism"). "There is no universe other than a human universe, the universe of human subjectivity," Sartre professed. And that basic fact requires humans to act on the world around them—to embrace their freedom to shape their own lives. You might recall that catchy phrase, "existence precedes essence," possibly uttered at some point by one of your college professors or ambitious high school teachers years ago. Well, in *essence*, that's the gist of Sartre's philosophy: "first of all, man exists, turns up, appears on the scene, and, only afterwards, defines himself. . . . Only afterward will he be something, and he himself will have made what he will be."

For Sartre, there isn't any sort of pre-existing essence characterizing humankind. Piper doesn't have any sort of preordained purpose in life. She's condemned to freely create her own purpose, to make her own existence meaningful and worthwhile amid all sorts of different choices she's going to be confronted with. Or, maybe she won't—but even *that* is a choice she will have to make. According to Sartre, "Man is nothing else but what he makes of himself," and this straightforward point is the "first principle" of the existential worldview.

Now, I know what you're thinking: "condemned" is a pretty strong word to use to describe Piper's life, even if she is currently serving a prison sentence. But, for existentialists like Sartre, that's exactly what she is: *condemned* to be free. It might sound a bit harsh, but when we think about it, we find, just like Sartre, that we didn't exactly create ourselves (I know I didn't, at least!). But, here we are. And that's his point: we've been "thrown into the world" and are responsible for everything we do. The full responsibility of our existence rests on us, Sartre argues. So, there's no sense in complaining about situations we ourselves are responsible for creating either; to do so would irresponsibly cast aside the guilt or regret we have created for ourselves, on our own. It's pretty obvious that Piper feels the same way, too.

During "WAC Pack," while Piper's mother, Carol, is reiterating what she thinks is obvious—Alex Vause is the reason Piper is there and is responsible for ruining this part of her life—Piper gives her a powerful reminder, something Sartre would have surely nodded his head to with a coy, little smile:

> Mom, . . . I need you to hear what I'm going to say. I need you to really hear it. I am in here, because I am no different from anybody else in here. I made bad choices. I committed a crime. And being in here is no one's fault but my own.

But, we all make bad choices from time to time, right? And some of us don't always get caught making those bad choices either, as the rookie guard Susan Fischer confesses to Piper in "Blood Donut": "I just want you to know that as far as I'm concerned, you and me are the same . . . the only difference between us is when I made bad decisions in life, I didn't get caught." What a sweet thing to tell an inmate in prison, no? But, sheesh . . . thanks for rubbing it in, Fischer.

Freedom Was Inconvenient for You?

Now, let's be honest: sometimes having all of this freedom isn't always as great and easy as it sounds. That *absolute* level of freedom and responsibility can definitely seem a little intimidating. Tasha "Taystee" Jefferson got out of prison early, only to find herself back in Litchfield once again. Complaining about how rough life outside of prison was for her in comparison to incarceration, her closest friend in the Litchfield prison, Poussey Washington, gave her a piece of her mind: "I know you ain't telling me in my face right now that you walked back in this place 'cuz freedom was inconvenient for you." Maybe Poussey was coming down a little hard on Taystee (hey, at least she gets a bed and regular meals each day in prison!). But, freedom is tough–especially for those who don't know how to handle the responsibility that comes with it. And, sometimes, that results in a denial of it.

One of the Issues Here Is Your Need to Say that a Person Is Exactly Anything

Sartre refers to that denial as "bad faith": when we deny our status as a conscious subject (a "being-for-itself") by assuming the identity of an absolute object (a "being-in-itself"—like a misplaced screwdriver or combination lock). He uses a famous example of a café waiter to show us the difference: one who is simply playing the role of a café waiter (but isn't defined by it) versus one who believes he *is* a café waiter (and is defined by it). There's a clear distinction between the two, and recognizing it seems to be one of Larry Bloom's problems as well. Piper's brother, Cal, points this out in "Fool Me Once" when Larry brings up the uncertain future of his relationship with Piper after finding out she's been having an affair with Alex:

> LARRY: So, what, is she gay now?
>
> CAL: I don't know about *now*. I just think that she is what she is, man.
>
> LARRY: Which is what, exactly?

CAL: I'm gonna go ahead and guess that one of the issues here is your need to say that a person is *exactly* anything.

We might be quick to dismiss Larry's troubled point of view, but it's not as easy to shake this perspective as we might think. And Larry isn't alone either.

We can see this confusion in both Galina "Red" Reznikov and Yvonne "Vee" Parker as well. When Red loses her position as head chef in the prison ("Can't Fix Crazy"), her whole world is turned upside down: she was the one in charge, smuggling in goods and gifts for her fellow inmates through a produce supplier and calling the shots with most of the inmates since she controlled *what* and *if* they ate. Now, she's just another inmate among the rest. She's noticeably feeling lost until she revives her position as a smuggler and provider (even managing to turn the greenhouse into a makeshift kitchen and dining room one evening). For Red, she *is* a chef. She *is* the head honcho (or, "mother" in the diverse "family" she has created).

Vee acts in much the same way when she returns to Litchfield during Season Two. She was a drug dealer and manipulator on the outside, and it isn't long until she revives that role while she's there— smuggling in tobacco and heroin. This role, Vee believes, defines who she *is*. And it's not just about the money either; it's "about making something of yourselves" she tells her new prison mules ("Comic Sans"). I'm not so sure that's the type of meaning and beauty Yoga Jones had in mind, but we can see both Red and Vee acting in bad faith in these instances—reducing their *being* to being in-itself, just like Sartre's confused café waiter.

Defender of the Unborn

When we act in bad faith, we not only deny our freedom and responsibility; we also make it very difficult to live an authentic, meaningful life. Simone de Beauvoir, Sartre's lifelong partner and fellow existentialist, expands on the various identities we might assume in bad faith in her *Ethics of Ambiguity*–the two particular freedom deniers being "sub-men" and "serious men." Pennsatucky actually displays these aspects of bad *faith* quite well, too (I hope you're catching the irony here).

She's currently serving a sentence for shooting an abortion clinic worker who "disrespected" her after conducting a fifth, consecutive abortion ("Number five, huh? We should give you a punch card . . . get the sixth one free."). Following her arrest, she's hailed as a "defender of the unborn" and embraced by Christian anti-abortion groups as a hero (but, come on, "Tiffany for President"?). Assuming this newfound identity, and aligning herself with its ideological claims, Pennsatucky recruits "converts" of her own in prison and regularly preaches to other inmates. But, is Pennsatucky acting authentically when she embraces her new identity as a Christian fundamentalist and defender of the unborn?

For de Beauvoir, the sub-man refuses to authentically cast himself into the world. Instead, he chooses to "take refuge" in its "ready-made values," and "take shelter behind a label" (pp. 43–44). Sound familiar? Naturally, de Beauvoir claims, this can lead to the path of the serious man when the sub-man "forces himself to submerge his freedom" in these values and labels. "He loses himself in the object in order to annihilate his subjectivity," de Beauvoir states (p. 45). In this way, he becomes enslaved by whatever these values are and adopts a willingness to sacrifice himself in their name.

It's pretty clear that Pennsatucky's new faith and role as an agent of God have taken the forefront of her existence. Based on the flashbacks throughout "Fool Me Once," we can be pretty sure that she couldn't have cared less until her "pro bono" lawyer decided to defend her crime as part of a holy cause and crusade against abortion. It's obvious that her "heroism" inflated her ego as she adopted this role, and the fan mail she apparently receives in prison certainly hasn't helped. And now, everything she does is in service to this evangelical and fundamentalist cause—which can apparently be advanced by violence, if necessary ("WAC Pack").

But we all know that Pennsatucky is trying to "make something" of her time at Litchfield—just like Piper and the others—regardless of the fact that it might be somewhat misdirected. We got a taste of what she's capable of doing with herself when she assisted Sam Healy in founding Safe Place ("Take a Break from Your Values"). We also noticed it when she took the kindness and compassion Healy taught her and applied it to making a new friend in Carrie "Big Boo" Black—someone she "would have never talked to" (even though part of that seems to have come from a curiosity in Healy's twisted notion of a "gay agenda" to "take over the world"). But, she's also still very much attached to the platform her lawyer set up, and how her actions will negatively affect her "allegiance" to God.

I Cannot Let Her Stay in Psych

While Piper does have her bouts of denial—like telling Larry she's not as independent as she had imagined ("Low Self Esteem City")—she's clearly taking steps in the right direction, embracing her choices and being responsible for her actions. We see a great example of this in "Tall Men with Feelings" after Piper thinks about that faith healing prank she helped play on Pennsatucky (which landed Ms. Doggett on the psychiatric ward—a place that is apparently much worse than solitary confinement): "I don't think that Pennsatucky deserves to be in psych. . . . It's pretty horrible . . . I am going to go to Caputo's office and I'm going to tell him that it was my fault and that he should let her out. . . . We did not play a prank on Pennsatucky. We were mean. I cannot let her stay in psych. I can't." In this scene, we watch Piper take charge of her life by doing what she feels is right, knowing that *she* is the one who has to make such a choice—one way or the other.

There Ain't No Judge

There obviously wasn't an appeal to a deity involved with her decision either—something we've been getting at this entire time. The secular humanist perspective is based on science, inquiry, and experiential truth—all of which are practically irrelevant when it comes to supernatural explanations and deities. Pennsatucky sums up what this missing feature might mean for the recently disillusioned theist near the end of Season One ("Fool Me Once"):

> Do you know what it means when there ain't nobody up there punishing evildoers? It means there ain't nobody giving out prizes for the good ones neither. 'Cuz there ain't no judge. There ain't no justice. We just crawl around this earth like ants. And then we die.

When no one is looking out for you, guiding and directing your behavior and choices, abandonment and loneliness might seem like obvious feelings to have—especially for theists like Pennsatucky.

This prospect could obviously be somewhat troubling, since it would seem that there are "no values or commands to turn to which legitimize our conduct," as Sartre states. Well, maybe there isn't some almighty judge laying down eternal punishments and handing out heavenly rewards (apparently, transportation buses to paradise are involved as well, according to Pennsatucky), but that certainly doesn't mean there isn't any justice. So, what is someone like Piper left to do? On what sort of model can she base her actions and values?

There's an obvious answer here: she should trust her instincts. We see Piper display this in the faith healing example above, and this sort of ethical approach aligns with the humanist attitude toward ethics: ethical values are based on and tested by our experiences and the needs of others, and moral standards "grow out of reflective inquiry" (*What Is Secular Humanism?*, p. 40). "Only a reflective decision," Kurtz states, "can best balance competing values and principles, or balance self-interest with the needs and demands of others." The humanist and existential perspective is grounded in individual freedom and responsibility, and that responsibility extends to others as well. The American Humanist Association's *Humanism and Its Aspirations* sums up this attitude:

> Humanists ground values in human welfare shaped by human circumstances, interests, and concerns and extended to the global ecosystem and beyond. We are committed to treating each person as having inherent worth and dignity, and to making informed choices in a context of freedom consonant with responsibility.

And for secular humanists like Piper Chapman, the existence of a supernatural being isn't required to act in this way.

I Need It to Be Real

According to Kurtz, secular humanists "find the classical definition of an omnipotent, omniscient, and beneficent God to be unintelligible, and the alleged proofs for God's existence inconclusive, and the problem of reconciling evil with presumptions of divine justice insurmountable" (p. 31). It's not that secular humanists like Piper are gung-ho about proving an ethical monotheistic deity doesn't exist (she hardly appears to have that agenda throughout the series); they're just interested in knowledge that can be verified and experientially proven one way or the other. And for "atheistic existentialists" like Sartre, that missing deity simply confirms our quest to define ourselves in this world and to embrace the responsibility that characterizes our freedom.

As we've seen, secular humanism is scientific in its efforts to understand the world. "Any 'theories of reality' are thus derived from the tested hypotheses and from theories rooted in scientific inquiry, rather than from poetic, literary, or theological narrations, interesting as these might be" (p. 28). And since proofs and explanations for God's existence come with a number of different verification problems, the secular humanist is left with no other choice but to disregard these cosmic variables until there's enough evidence to address them. But, that functional quality Piper hints at—that religion might help make things easier to deal with and help people remain "happy"—can also prevent people from acting authentically in the world, denying their freedom and responsibility.

Karl Marx has become rather well-known in religious studies circles for his "opium" analogy: religion functions as an "opium" for oppressed people, keeping them "happy" and preventing them from trying to make something better for themselves. And just like Marx, Piper recognizes that religion can help those who are living pretty crummy lives feel better. But, for secular humanists, that feeling is superficial, fleeting, and can have devastating results, even if it feels great—much like opium. For Marx, these types of beliefs provide people with a form of illusory happiness; finding refuge in this "happiness" and the understanding that there's a reward waiting for them on the other side, people are less inclined to take charge of their destinies and work towards ridding themselves of the horrible conditions in which they're living.

A demand for real happiness, in the Marxian sense, would be the strive towards freedom, responsibility, and authenticity that we see in Piper as she struggles to emerge from Litchfield with a new orientation to the world around her. What we also see in Piper is that, contrary to Ms. Doggett, theistic beliefs aren't required for a meaningful existence and don't make the secular humanist outlook any less meaningful as a result.

And those types of unscientific and unverifiable beliefs might even be counterproductive themselves. The thought that there is some sort of supernatural fatherly figure looking out for us does sound a bit comforting—especially in those instances when we're feeling a bit abandoned or lonely, like in prison. But, that warm, fuzzy feeling isn't enough to satisfy secular humanists like Piper Chapman. She has a responsibility to deal with certain things in her life as she tries to make it meaningful and beautiful. And she needs them to be *real*.

VI

The secret is, pretend the salt is sugar

11
I Am I, Crazy Eyes

Chelsi Barnard Archibald

Suzanne Warren (a.k.a. "Crazy Eyes") is a lot like René Descartes, the father of modern philosophy. They both continuously doubt everything they've been brought up to believe, constantly questioning their surroundings and the evidence of their senses.

Their motives are a bit different though. Descartes's motivation for challenging the world as he found it is quite different from Suzanne's. Descartes wants to have a firm foundation for all knowledge—both practical, common-sense knowledge and the sciences.

Descartes decided that the best way to get at this firm foundation was to begin by doubting absolutely everything, then trying to come up with something that could not possibly be doubted. As part of his general method of calling as much into doubt as could possibly be doubted, he imagined that there was a very powerful evil demon who was determined to deceive him by feeding him false sights and sounds, so that the world Descartes thought he could perceive was actually no more real than a dream.

The imaginative features of experience are the ones that resonate most with Crazy Eyes. Her understanding of the world is very different from the way that others understand it, as her behavior in the prison frequently demonstrates.

When Suzanne's backstory is revealed, we learn that she was adopted and grew up a troubled child. Her imaginative nature and penchant for seeing the world differently was always difficult for her parents deal with. Throughout her childhood, her mother constantly tried to create a foundation of normalcy in which Suzanne could thrive, but Suzanne retreats to the safety of her imagination. She was a fantastical child who wore fairy wings daily. On one particular occasion that we see in a flashback, she visits the hospital to see her new baby sister and she says, "Can I hold the miracle?" Suzanne sees everything as having great purpose, and to her, a new baby is nothing short of a miracle. However, when her father starts to worry about her overzealous excitement for the baby he takes it away leaving Suzanne to exclaim, "No! She is my baby! Give her back!" From that time forward, Suzanne is constantly thrown between two worlds, one in which her noble pursuits generated, in part, by her active imaginative life can be played out, and the other in which she must question everything in her surroundings for ultimate truth.

Starting from Scratch

Major changes were occurring in the world in which Descartes lived. As a result of the Protestant Reformation in the sixteenth century, people went from a feeling of absolute certainty in God and other traditional beliefs, to a growing sense of doubt and a willingness to question what had previously been taken for granted.

Descartes wanted a systematic approach to knowing for certain what is real and what is not real. He believed in a rigorous questioning of everything and an application of heavy skepticism. He believed that by doubting everything, he could find those things which are beyond doubt, and use these as first principles, from which, by the use of reason, he could attain further knowledge. Descartes believed he had found that firm foundation of all knowledge in the statement, 'I think, therefore I am'. While I can doubt almost everything, I cannot doubt that I exist, because I cannot doubt that I am now having a thought.

Descartes believed it was vital to hold our own critical beliefs up to an intense skeptical scrutiny because simply by living and participating in society, one is heavily conditioned to hold any number of false beliefs. This conditioning leads to things that are unhealthy and unproductive—aspects of society, organizations, or religions that might cause us harm or that might prevent us from living our lives fully. While Suzanne's mother meant well by pressuring her to join institutions of normalcy, like school clubs, church groups, and social interactions with popular girls in her neighborhood, it was ultimately something that created a larger challenge for Suzanne. It mixed up her sense of what truth really was.

Descartes also believed that if there is even an ounce of uncertainty or a shadow of a doubt, then a person is obligated to throw out any previous notions or beliefs they once had and start again from the beginning. In certain respects, Suzanne seems to try to follow Descartes's general strategy. She tends to constantly question herself and the truth of what seems to be happening in the world. While this may seem as though she is unsure, she is actually trying to gain balance in deciphering the difference between her noble world and the unworthy world of darkness trying to bring her down.

Descartes explained that thoughts based on what we're accustomed to believe are like a barrel of apples in which a few may be poisonous. The only way to be certain that a poisoned apple will not be one's undoing is to throw out the entire batch and start anew. One biased thought formed due to human conditioning could essentially pollute the rest of the ideas a person could have. It's better to throw out all beliefs rather than entertain anything untrue. The philosopher often reflected on the number of falsehoods he had believed during his lifetime. In his *Meditations*, he breaks down the Aristotelian notion that all knowledge comes from the senses and draws a distinction between the mind and the body. The mind is a thinking entity while the body is a feeling entity, an extension of the mind.

> I must once and for all seriously undertake to rid myself of all the opinions which I had formerly accepted, and commence to build anew from the foundation, if I wanted to establish any firm and permanent structure in the sciences. (*Meditations*, p. 5)

Many times when Suzanne is having trouble adapting to a current situation or lacks the ability to ground herself in the reality of her choosing, she starts to hit herself repeatedly in order to reset her brain. This kind of ritual is far from the secluded method of contemplation that Descartes engaged in, but we can understand it as Suzanne's attempt to do as Descartes would do—throw out prior notions and trying to begin from scratch.

Tilting at a Windmill

When Suzanne is ten she attends a birthday party for her little sister's friend. The girl's mother tries to deny

Suzanne entrance. Suzanne's mother wants her adopted daughter to have the same social developments as Grace, even though she is a few years older than the little girls at the party. The neighbor finds it inappropriate, but after being lectured by Suzanne's mother, she relents.

The girls at the party change into their pajamas and an already prepubescent developing Suzanne takes off her bra discretely reminding her sister that she's "not weird" for having to do so. The girls start a story-telling game in which each person adds a part to the story. When it's Suzanne's turn she adds a dragon to the story, which burns down the house of the princess and leaves her unable to be saved by anyone, alone, and crying. The other girls are horrified. One even calls Suzanne's dragon "stupid" to which she replies, "But dragons are cool!"

In 1614, when Descartes was eighteen years old, Miguel de Cervantes published his novel *Don Quixote*, in which the knight Don Quixote continually misinterprets what's going on around him, and this story of fanciful delusion heavily influenced the young Descartes. We can understand Crazy Eyes as *Orange Is the New Black*'s Don Quixote character. There are pros and cons to this similarity when it comes to survival inside of Litchfield Penitentiary.

Descartes's understanding of the workings of the mind acknowledges that the imagination plays some role in conceiving of possibilities and even in the practice of formulating the very skeptical scenarios that make it possible for us to call our beliefs into doubt. He also sees imagination, taken together with will, as a potential source of false beliefs. Our imagination may create possibilities that extend past those that are really present in reality, and we then willfully accept those possibilities *as* reality. So, while the imagination is useful, it is also dangerous.

By contrast, Cervantes sees the imagination quite differently. He might support Suzanne's need to make the world more noble and bigger than the reality presented. Don Quixote uses imagination to overcome frightful situations, for example, when thieves attack him and his companion Sancho. For Quixote, viewing everything through the lens of his imagination is crucial to his survival, because it never fails him. Like Suzanne, he is capable of overcoming any "danger" because the appearance of any obstacle is inconsequential. Neither Quixote nor Suzanne relies on everyday normal people or leaders to guide their ideas and so when they are threatened their senses do not react normally at all. In fact, both characters flourish under these circumstances and stay mentally safe.

Rationalists and Other Prisoners

Descartes's need to break everything down and start from scratch created a dichotomy in the philosophical world, between rationalism and empiricism. Rationalism is the view that we gain knowledge in significant ways through the use of reason alone. Empiricism is the view that the knowledge ultimately derives from sense experience. Though he might not ever have the certainty that he claims, Don Quixote is driven by noble ideals, ethical imperatives, and an absolute sense of certainty, even when the things he takes to be true are inconsistent with the facts of his sense experience. In a way then, we might say that Don Quixote is in the rationalist tradition. He believes that he can know significant things about upright moral behavior such as chivalry and noble behavior by reflecting on the nature of those concepts themselves. This is true even when the facts of his situation seem to diverge from his lofty judgments about them. Consider Don Quixote's description of Dulcinea, the woman for whom he valiantly fights. He describes her in the following way:

> Her name is Dulcinea, her country El Toboso, a village of La Mancha, her rank must be at least that of a princess, since she is my queen and lady, and her beauty superhuman, since all the impossible and fanciful attributes of beauty which the poets apply to their ladies are verified in her; for her hairs are gold, her forehead Elysian fields, her eyebrows rainbows, her eyes suns, her cheeks roses, her lips coral, her teeth pearls, her neck alabaster, her bosom marble, her hands ivory, her fairness snow, and what modesty conceals from sight such, I think and imagine, as rational reflection can only extol, not compare. (Volume 1, Chapter XIII)

Don Quixote has idealized the woman that he has only met on one or two occasions. His companion, Sancho, by contrast, describes Dulcinea in the following way:

> I can tell you that she pitches a bar as well as the strongest lad in the whole village... She's a brawny girl, well built and tall and sturdy, and she will know how to keep her chin out of the mud with any knight errant who ever has her for his mistress. O the wench, what muscles she's got, and what a pair of lungs! I remember the day she went up the village belfry to call in some of their lads who were working in a fallow field of her father's, and they could hear her plainly as if they had been at the foot of the tower, although they were nearly two miles away. There's a good deal of the court-lady about her too, for she has a crack with everybody, and makes a joke and a mock of them all. (Volume 1, Chapter XXV)

145

Suzanne's attitudes are more like those of Don Quixote. In an environment that is often very harsh, she tries to maintain a grasp on ideals she has internalized. For example, she quotes Shakespeare, upholds chivalry, and writes poetry. In her unique way, she comes to conclusions as to who is proper or not proper at Litchfield. As soon as Piper arrives at Litchfield, though Suzanne doesn't know her at all, she uses what she takes to be her innate sense of nobility and justice to assess Piper as "a lady," referring to her as her "Dandelion."

Suzanne uses her intuition and what she takes to be an innate apprehension of truth without ever needing to rely on the senses. Ideas of romantic love, chivalry, and the lifting up the female figure are things that Quixote and Suzanne have in common. For example, after helping Piper obtain some peppers to concoct a cream for Red's back and regain her favor as well as the ability to eat lunch again, Suzanne feels like she's aiding a great lady in distress and the service is a higher calling of protection and gallantry. When Piper expresses her appreciation for the peppers at what she perceives as a friendly gesture, Suzanne then sits near her during movie time, shares her headphones with her, and sweetly holds Piper's hand.

She later tells Piper, "You're a real woman. A real grown woman," as the two walk outside in the prison yard. She recites poetry to her that she wrote herself. Later on, Suzanne rescues Piper from Alex's advances in the lunchroom by throwing her pie and threatening to hurt the woman intruding on her territory saying later, "I have feelings. Love feelings."

In Suzanne's eyes Piper can be considered both her Sancho and her Dulcinea, a lady of high birth. Piper shows her classicism in various ways, by owning a luxury soap start-up company and doing a cleanse, eating hardly anything in order to lose weight, all prior to landing in prison.

Quixote's partner Sancho is similar to Piper in that he straddles two worlds. He represents the empiricist attitude of observant, moderate, pragmatism. Like the other prisoners, Piper can be prone to giving into the senses, living life through an individual lens of experience and individual needs as well as using inductive reasoning, and making generalizations based solely on individual instances. While Suzanne feels like her purpose in life is innate and her talents come from something beyond her, her fellow inmates focus on the day-to-day drudgery of their individual perception.

Though both Don Quixote and Suzanne seem to have rationalist ways of looking at the world, in both cases something has gone wrong. But in another respect, perhaps there are some things that have gone right. On the one hand, there is a sense in which we all want to say that both Crazy Eyes and Don Quixote are nuts. They are guided by their internal sense of good, right and wrong, noble and vulgar. The truth of the matter, unfortunately, is that their judgments in the cases in which they find themselves don't turn out to be accurate (consider Suzanne's obsessive devotion to Vee, even in light of overwhelming empirical evidence that Vee is an evil, manipulative person).

Descartes's assessment of what has gone wrong here would likely have something to do with his discussion of the mind and its component parts. Imagination appears to be playing a strong role both with regard to Don Quixote and to Suzanne. They both have genuine objects of affection, but they have used their imagination to extend the virtues of their beloveds beyond what is actually true. In both of these cases, the human capacity of imagination and the faculty of will have lead

Don Quixote and Crazy Eyes astray. They willfully choose to believe the outputs of imagination that go beyond the reality of the situation. As a result, they have false beliefs, and false beliefs can hurt when they are discovered.

On the other hand, truth may not be all that matters. The imagination helps create beauty, honor, and nobility in situations in which such features do not already exist. Prison is an ugly place. Perhaps a little imagination could make it better.

The Evil Demon Made Me Do It

Romantic love is a serious endeavor for Suzanne, and like Don Quixote she does not take it well when Piper slights her. She requests to bunk with her, but is swiftly rejected making her realize that Piper is undeserving of her love. "This year I'm loving someone who deserves me," she says. Suzanne then urinates in Piper's cellblock. When asked later about her ideal of romantic love she states:

> It's like you become more you . . . Because the person, like, whoever, they chose to take that on. All of that weird stuff. But now it's okay. Whatever is wrong or bad or hiding in you, suddenly it's all right. You don't feel like such a freak anymore.

Like Descartes, Quixote imagines that an evil enchanter works constantly for his undoing and the demon also focuses on shaking the confidence of the host's cognitive faculties. Quixote and Suzanne are two characters that give us a concrete example of what it would be like to try and live in the radical world of the skeptic, denying the environment around us. They distrust everything and refuse to see negativity or that which is less than noble, which causes them to turn inward and reside in a world that does not betray them.

William Egginton suggests that in the eyes of people like Quixote and Suzanne, there are hordes of enchanters always walking among us and altering or changing everything. Thus Suzanne mentions inner "freak" when she speaks of what true love means to her.

For Suzanne, even the task of mopping the bathroom floor takes on a higher calling. "Sometimes the feelings inside of me get messy like dirt and I like to clean things and the dirt is the feelings. The floor is my mind. That is called 'coping'," she tells Piper. ("Fool Me Once")

Later on, Suzanne reminds Piper how loyal she was to her and tells her that she is a mean person and should think about becoming better. "You gotta start from the inside-out or else you'll step on the clean," Suzanne says. The tasks she is given at Litchfield are not simple to her nor are they unimportant, they are a metaphor for her to live her life by and she sees them as objects to conquer, just like she sees Piper as a noble woman who must act like a lady. In Suzanne's eyes, this does not include "mean" behavior.

Suzanne approaches life rather like an actor who memorizes and practices a role. Where some often see Quixote as a madman others consider him a clever genius that is merely playing a part in order to avoid the world. While watching Suzanne, one often questions whether she is deliberately putting on an act of insanity or is in fact, truly insane. When a group of troublesome youth is brought to the prison for a "Scared Straight!" program, Suzanne becomes excited at the chance to play a worthy role. "I wanna play a role like Ophelia, Desdemona, Clair Huxtable," she exclaims.

Suzanne embraces her chosen role as Coriolanus, Shakespeare's tragic military general in Rome who is disgusted by the status quo and she spouts into the youth's faces, "You common cry of curs! Whose breath I hate as reek o' the rotten fens. Whose loves I prize, that do corrupt my air!" It is interesting that Suzanne would choose this series of lines to quote as Coriolanus is not considered suited for politics and refuses to play the same game as the people around him. This is very similar to Suzanne's approach to dealing with life in prison. She elevates herself above the fray by acting as if her life is only involved with noble pursuits like true love, rescuing damsels in distress, or denying the ugliness of the world.

Suzanne copes with an unkind and ugly world by seeing everything as a play. When Vee is ignored by Taystee, Suzanne reassures her not to take it personally. "You gotta put your head down buffing those floors. Sometimes people just don't want to play with you and that's okay." Suzanne is able to rise above the prison squabbles mainly because she is used to being left out and because she prefers her own endeavors. When Taystee, Poussey, and their friends play charades Suzanne is happy to take on the role of timekeeper and watches the clock diligently. They see her as simple-minded, but she understands the importance of someone holding the entire structure of the game together.

The main motivating force behind the actions of Don Quixote is his need to do justice in the world and to find truth, and he therefore follows a knightly code that demands truthful behavior. Oftentimes, those around him question his adherence to this imaginary world. As is the case for Suzanne, her faith is strength enough and reality is always weaker.

Cervantes will sometimes use the Don's current situation to show how his meddlesomeness can result in the undoing of those he would wish to help. Suzanne desires to help others and does not come off as a selfish person. Any trouble that she may get into she does from a good place in her heart, an example being the horrible favors she does for Vee. When Poussey becomes depressed and severely drunk because Vee has separated her from her girlfriend Taystee, she insults Vee.

Earlier in the series when Vee arrived she quickly saw the power in Suzanne's need to be special and to be recognized, saying to her, "Everyone else here underestimates you." This is the manipulative validation that Suzanne craves and it is also the first time someone in the series calls her by her real name, "Suzanne," rather than her pseudonym "Crazy Eyes." She expresses early on "I am not crazy. I am unique . . . How come everyone calls me 'Crazy Eyes'?" In return for Vee's recognition of her as a person rather than a crazy person, Suzanne devotes herself to Vee like she would a royal queen, corrupt as Vee may be. Poussey feels the brunt of Suzanne's wrath at her Queen Vee being insulted and beats the poor girl in a fit of rage.

I Imagine, Therefore I Am

For Descartes, sensation, imagination, memory, and pure understanding were all capacities of a single mind. These capacities were distinguished from one another on the basis of their function. For example, sense perception involves receiving impressions from the external world through the sense organs, much in the same way in which a seal makes an impression on a piece of wax. Descartes's conception of the way the mind works is very different from the way that we conceive of it today. According to his view, animal spirits are sent through the fibers that comprise the brain via a pattern distinctive of the content of the sense experience. These impressions are sent to an area of the brain called the common sense. The common sense, as the name suggests, is an area of the brain that can process in various ways information obtained by all of the sense organs in common.

One way that information obtained through the senses can be utilized is by the faculty of imagination. In the early modern era of philosophy, "imagination" did not have the same connotation that it does today. It is common today to attribute heightened imagination to a person if they are uncommonly inventive, creative, or resourceful. Although one could certainly engage in these sorts of behaviors when exercising one's imagination in the early modern sense, imagination at that time was understood as the faculty responsible for combining information obtained through the senses in various ways. These ways may be unique and creative or they may correspond to the way things are in the external world. For example, the imagination would be active if one pictured various parts of different animals as coming together to form a single animal, such as a hippogryph or a sphinx. Imagination might also be active when I think about the glass that I left in the kitchen—in this case my imagination constructs the scene as it really is.

Imagination does not require the objects that produce the sense experience to be actually present at the time when they are imagined. Imaginings, then, do not always produce knowledge of the external world because the things imagined may or may not exist in the external world at the time at which they are imagined. Imagination presents us only with possibilities, not with realities. As a result, imagination generates some of the skeptical problems in Descartes's *Meditations*. It is imagination that, in the case of madmen, causes them

> to assert that they are monarchs when they are in the greatest poverty; or clothed in gold and purple when destitute of any covering; or that their head is made of clay, their body of glass, or that they are gourds. (p. 5)

The problem is, imagination allows us to consider sensory possibilities, but cannot itself check to see whether any particular possibility corresponds with the truth. There are situations in which one takes simple imaginings as truth, such as when one is mad or dreaming. If one cannot distinguish such situations from situations in which one really is receiving information from the external world, the imagination presents a problem for knowledge.

Though imagination and sensation are properties of the mind, they have a different status from pure understanding or intellect. Imagination and sensation, are properties of the mind, but are not essential properties of the mind. Mind can exist without the properties of imagination and sensation, but imagination and sensation cannot exist without existing in some intellectual substance. In the sixth meditation, Descartes says:

> I find in myself faculties for certain special modes of thinking, namely imagination and sensory perception. Now I can clearly and distinctly understand myself as a whole without these faculties; but I cannot, conversely, understand these faculties without me, that is, without an intellectual substance to inhere in.

A feature that is crucial to mind is intellect or pure understanding. This is the capacity that allows Descartes to determine those things that he clearly and distinctly perceives. It is a capacity that involves reflection. On the difference between the capacities of imagination and pure understanding, Descartes says:

> Thus this way of thinking [imagining] differs from pure understanding only in the sense that the mind, when it understands, turns back on itself in some way and reflects on one of the ideas that are inside itself; however, when it imagines, it turns toward a body and sees something in it that resembles the idea that had been understood by itself or perceived by sensation. (p. 58)

Getting the Dragons to Change Their Perspectives

Cervantes shows the futility of impetuously intruding into people's lives and Suzanne acts this out perfectly. Suzanne, like Quixote, yearns to help others to see the world as she sees it. At one particular lunch when the inmates food is over-salted and Taystee thinks the Latina cooks are doing it to the African American clique on purpose, Suzanne overlooks the clique wars and simply says, "The secret is to pretend the salt is sugar." While everyone ignores this declaration and most viewers see it merely as a quirky humorous aspect of Crazy Eyes's character, it is clear that in Suzanne's view there is a deeper meaning to acting as though a horrible world is wonderful.

Suzanne is also juxtaposed against the other inmates at Litchfield. Although the basic beliefs of the common prisoner are tenets of faith (be they conditioned biases), their imaginations are so circumscribed that they cannot understand anything else outside the box. Suzanne breaks this barrier. Her real enemy is not the prisoners, the time she is serving for her crime, or the prison itself, but instead her nemesis is the prosaic unimaginative world and the individuals who reside in such a world and refuse to see what she sees.

In Cervantes's adventure, the Don comes across "giants" or what Sancho recognizes as windmills. When Sancho points out their true form to Quixote he blames the change in form on the necromancer, always waiting to deceive him and divert him from his noble path. The same can be said for Suzanne who near the end of Season Two takes the blame for Red's attack when in fact, Vee is the true culprit. Healey points out to her that it's obvious that she was not the one to commit the attack and she becomes confused. "But who can I trust?" she asks Healey. "Yourself," he says. "Nooo!" she screams while hitting herself, feeling deceived once again by the evil genius inside of her head.

In Quixote's case it does not matter whether the ponderous windmill stands for stultified human enemies that need attacking or situations that must be questioned. The only positive act of will is the courage to act when the act is required, to do what is right, even if it is unfair or unjust to the self. In order to prove that he is living out his own reality authentically he must follow through no matter how often that reality is challenged. "Thy triumph was ever a triumph of daring, not of succeeding," Sancho tells his friend.

In the cases of both Don Quixote and Crazy Eyes, imagination is a powerful tool. It can lead those who blindly follow it astray, but it also has certain practical applications. Descartes's purpose was to find a foundation for knowledge and, ultimately, for the sciences. But there are other purposes, one of which may be to survive and even to thrive in a world that is not always a joyful place to be.

Specifically, in the case of Crazy Eyes, her imagination may keep her sane (or as sane as someone like her can be). Though it may lead to false beliefs, it also helps her to cope with the danger and unpleasantness of prison life.

12
You Got Them TV Titties

STEPHEN FELDER

Orange Is the New Black begins with the most ubiquitous cliché from the women-in-prison genre: the shower scene. Piper, wearing shower sandals she's constructed from Maxipads, is huddled in the shower when Taystee approaches her and, after hurrying her up a bit, pulls her towel back and tells her "Ooooh, you got some nice titties. . . You got them TV titties."

The scene introduces us to the way in which several of the actresses in the scene are subjected to the viewers' voyeuristic gaze in ways just as intrusive as Taystee's. Still, the scene does introduce us rapidly and effectively to the characters, situations, and themes that will become central occupations of the show. Among these themes is *the relationship between the self, the body, and the other.*

In philosophy, these issues have often been seen as involving the so-called "mind-body" problem. My body is a physical object, yet there is this other part of me—mind, spirit, consciousness, whatever you want to call it—that seems to be more than my body.

At least two kinds of questions emerge from this realization. The first has to do with human nature itself.

What kinds of things are we? Are we bodies? Are we minds? What's the relationship between the two? The second problem is sometimes framed as the "problem of other minds." It's the idea that the only mind I can be sure exists is my own. I can see other human bodies, but I don't know what is really going on inside of them. Since consciousness seems to be private, how can I know that what I experience when I see orange is the same experience you have of orange?

This isn't merely an epistemological problem (a problem concerning what's knowable); it extends to my relationships with other people because I confront their bodies as physical objects while their consciousness seems hidden and mysterious. This means that the other person, as a body, can tend to be an object for me. For some philosophers the terms "subject" and "object" have become a kind of short-hand, or jargon, for expressing this dynamic. We can understand these terms better if we consider them in their normal, grammatical sense. The "subject" is the agent performing the action of the verb in a sentence. The "object" is to whom, or for whom, something is done. In terms of the mind-body problem as it relates to the "other," the self is the subject who sees, acts, perceives, while the other is the object that is seen, acted upon, and perceived. When cast in terms of the mind-body problem, there is a tendency for us to think that we, who have access to our own conscious states, are always the "subject," and the other, whose consciousness remains concealed, but whose body is visible to me, is the object.

The shower scene between Piper and Taystee illustrates this dynamic. In this scene we mostly sense Piper being looked at by Taystee. It is Piper—her body, her "TV titties"—that are "objectified" under Taystee's gaze. At this moment Piper becomes aware of herself as an object. This seems to be one of the purposes of the scene, to show how the prison setting is dehumanizing, which is to say, how it turns "persons" with minds, souls, or selves into objects.

These issues were of great concern to two twentieth-century French philosophers, Jean-Paul Sartre (1905–1980) and Maurice Merleau-Ponty (1908–1961). For Sartre, the default situation for the self and other is one of alienation. My experiences of shame and fear point to the nature of this relationship and indicate the ways in which "the other" tends to be viewed as obstacle or tool. For Merleau-Ponty our default situation is one of connection with others, something he sometimes calls, "intersubjectivity." Much in Sartre's account is compelling, especially in the ways he explains our experiences of shame and fear, but ultimately, as *Orange Is the New Black* illustrates, Merleau-Ponty's account is more perceptive, uncovering both what is problematic in Sartre's theory and what is promising about his own way of dissolving the problem of other minds.

Sartre on Why Hugs Can Be Deceiving

For Sartre, my normal orientation towards the world is one of a subject confronting a world of objects towards which I have intentions. To be a subject—to be a "self"—requires "a refusal of the Other" (*Being and Nothingness*, p. 377). When I encounter other people, that is, when I see their bodies, hear their voices, sense their presence, only one of two possibilities is open to me: either I encounter that person as an object—as obstacle or tool towards my own goals—or I feel the other treating me in the same way, in which case I cease to be what Sartre calls a "for itself" (a subject) and become an "in-itself" (an object). When I see another person, because I don't have direct access to that person's consciousness, I don't see her as a subject with her own possibilities and plans, rather I see her as either an instrument to achieve some goal of mine (sexual pleasure, hair-care products, cigarettes) or as an obstacle (might cheat on me, hide my mattress, stab me with a cross).

Thus, according to Sartre, I am in a nearly constant state of being an object for others who are, in turn, objects for me. But, according to Sartre, there are special cases when the "gaze of the other" can convert me into an object for myself. Sartre uses the example of someone who is staring through a keyhole and suddenly hears someone behind him. This awareness of being looked at by another evokes an experience of "shame." Something like this happens when Pornstache emerges from a utility closet where he has obviously been extorting sex from Leanne only to be "caught" by Burset. Burset's gaze awakens a self-consciousness in Pornstache in the form of shame ("Lesbian Request Denied").

While shame is one situation in which this phenomenon is particularly clear, according to Sartre, fear and vanity can have the same effect. In fear, I am aware of myself as an object for the other who may do me harm, like when Piper is aware that Pennsatucky wants to kill her. Sartre thinks of vanity as another example, like when Burset sees herself in the mirror in ways that suggest she is imagining herself as an object for another. Sartre argues that it is through these experiences that an awareness of myself as a self emerges. His formula for this is to say that when I feel shame "*I am ashamed of myself before the Other*" (p. 385).

In this formulation the three terms—"I," "myself," and "the Other"—form a sort of consciousness mirror in which I see myself being looked at by the Other who is being looked at by me. For Sartre, this gaze of the other, which he sees as so crucial for self-consciousness, comes at the cost of becoming an "object" for myself. He argues the remedy for this is to subject the other to my objectifying gaze, restoring my place as the subject. This is what Pornstache does to Burset when he's caught extorting sex from Leanne. Instead of submitting to the shame-inducing gaze of Burset, Pornstache reverses the dynamic with a fear-inducing gaze.

Thus, for Sartre, intersubjectivity (the experience of connection with another person's consciousness) is inherently unstable, and the experience of self-consciousness is inevitably alienating, since it involves either seeing others as objects or being seen as an object myself.

There are many features of Sartre's understanding of the gaze of the Other that seem, at least intuitively, to make sense of the world. All of us can relate to the feelings of shame and fear explained by his theory. We have all had moments where we could feel ourselves being looked at by another person in ways that evoked fear or shame, and we have all had concerns about being treated as objects.

A Body Gets Lonely in Here

But while there is much in *Orange Is the New Black* to confirm Sartre's thesis, a closer look reveals several problems. Merleau-Ponty pointed out some of those problems and argued for a third way of understanding the mind-body problem that dissolved the tensions inherent Sartre's understanding of being-for-itself (subject/observer) and being-in-itself (object/observed). For Merleau-Ponty being-in-the-world involves an *incarnated subjectivity* that affirms the fact that we are always both observer and observed, touched and touching, subject and object. But because we are always subject and object, we are a special kind of object—a body that is capable of being both seen and seeing. To describe our existence as "incarnated subjectivity" is to emphasize that our consciousness is not separate from our bodies, but somehow tied up with them. Our consciousness is not *inside* our flesh, it is *in the flesh itself.* In this view, to treat the "other" as object is to renounce our shared being-in-the-world, a shared being that results from this shared incarnated subjectivity.

In the shower scene between Piper and Taystee we can see that there are at least two ways in which the scene subverts Sartre's analysis in favor of Merleau-Ponty's. First, after the encounter with Taystee, as Piper walks off, she pulls her towel away and observes her own breasts, smiling, apparently in agreement with Taystee's appraisal. The intelligibility of Taystee's assessment of Piper's body is possible only because Piper and Taystee have a shared experience of observing breasts on television (hence the phrase, "TV titties"), and the fact that Piper, too, can observe her own breasts from Taystee's perspective implying a sort of "seeing-with." By "seeing with" I mean that it's not a matter of Piper seeing her own breasts as an object for Taystee who is a subject, but it is a matter of Piper, who is also a subject, seeing her own breasts *with* Taystee.

We could point out that the phenomenon occurring between Piper and Taystee is also occurring for the audience. We share a world that includes "TV titties," and we share bodies, not unlike Piper's and Taystee's, that both perceive and are perceived in ways very much like Piper's and Taystee's. Furthermore, we share experiences of evaluating ourselves in terms prescribed by our culture and assessed by others—an assessment which we are capable of enacting on ourselves because, and this is the key, we are relatively certain that our perceptions are roughly the same as those of others. The scene makes sense to us, as the audience, because our perceptions, are somehow not only *like* Piper's and Taystee's, but also *engaged with* theirs.

While the opening scene in *Orange Is the New Black* certainly does reproduce the dehumanizing situation of prison—that it is a situation in which people, subjects, are treated like objects—it also reminds us that this is not the only (nor the primordial) experience we have of our bodies in relationship to the gaze of others. The scene began with Piper's voice-over claiming she has "always loved getting clean . . . baths . . . showers . . ." It's her "happy place." This narration takes place over scenes of her bathing with Alex and Larry. This highlights that what is dehumanizing about the shower scene is not the exposure of the body to a *necessarily* objectifying and alienating gaze (Sartre's position), but that the prison shower represents *a departure* from more primary scenarios in which Piper has found joy in her being/bathing with, and being seen by, others (Merleau-Ponty's position).

We can say something similar about the objectifying gaze of Pornstache when Piper is changing her bra ("Lesbian Request Denied"). Yes, Pornstache is objectifying Piper with his gaze, and yes, she is feeling herself becoming an object, but something else is going on, too. We, as the viewers, are feeling that objectifying gaze as well. We feel it not because Pornstache is looking at us, but because we're looking at Piper being looked at by Pornstache and we *know* what it is to feel that kind of look. In that moment, we have access to Piper's consciousness (brought to life for us by Taylor Schilling) because we see Piper, and not because we are being seen (by Pornstache).

Merleau-Ponty and the SHU

We might object that while Merleau-Ponty's theory might give us a better understanding of how we relate to "the other," it doesn't actually solve the problem of other minds because we're just inferring Piper's feelings by analogy to our own experience. We have no guarantee that what Piper is experiencing is actually what we have experienced in similar circumstances because, as the problem of other minds tells us, we have no access to Piper's private experience. Since our experiences are ultimately private, isn't our situation solipsistic? Isn't everybody, in some sense, living in the SHU?

Merleau-Ponty's position addresses this problem by pointing out that my reason for believing my experiences are similar to yours is because, as we have seen, we have very similar bodies. While I can't literally compare my experience of orange with your experience of orange, I can assume that my experiences seem to more or less approximate yours. I assume this not because I have access to your private experience of color, but because my body, my eyes, my limbs, etc. are very much like yours and seem to operate the same way as yours. Our bodies, all more or less the same, seem equally at home in this world. You can ask me if I hear that bird, or see that cloud that looks like a bird, or feel the drops of rain as they begin to fall, and in each case you can reasonably expect that my body will respond to all these things in very much the same way as yours.

The same thing happens when we, as the audience, are streaming *Orange Is the New Black*. The fact that we can even engage with TV characters as somehow conveying experience suggests this kind of shared, bodily, being-at-home in the world. Piper (the character), Taylor Schilling (the actress), and I (the viewer) all have similar bodies, that function in similar ways, and that are similarly at home in the world, able to get around in it in much the same way. Therefore, Taylor Schilling can draw on our common experience of more-or-less similar bodies being similarly at home in a more-or-less-similar world to convey Piper's experience to us in a way that is immediately comprehensible to us.

This is also true when it comes to the objects that surround us. Merleau-Ponty explains that when I see objects around another person I understand those objects present possibilities not only for me, but also for the other. When I see a screwdriver I recognize that it's an object—tool, weapon, makeshift dildo—not only for me, but also for other humans whose bodies are like mine. This is why, Merleau-Ponty says, "it is precisely my body that perceives the other's body and finds there something of a miraculous extension of its own intentions, a familiar manner of handling the world" (*Phenomenology of Perception*, p. 370). Since it's my body that perceives the world (as opposed to some private consciousness) I can have general certainty that your perceptions and experiences with your body are similar to my own.

Instead of thinking of an "I" that is "inside" my body being confronted by objects "outside," Merleau-Ponty suggests that we think of consciousness as bodily and somehow immersed in a world of objects (and others) that gives this consciousness its shape. These objects can influence the way I touch them, or see them, or orient my entire body to get a better look, or feel to them. Bernard Flynn, explaining Merleau-Ponty's view, offers the excellent example of the experience we have when we want to touch the cloth of a coat we are considering buying. We don't pound the fabric with our fists, nor do we whisk our hand over it; instead, we, in Flynn's words, touch the cloth "as it wishes to be touched." As Flynn points out, "my body needs no instruction" in order to know how to feel the cloth in that kind of situation. The intention is in my body *and the cloth.*

Similarly, while we can take classes and read books on the appropriate techniques for sex and combat, isn't there something more immediate, more authentic, about the way Piper's body knows how to touch Alex's to produce pleasure and connection, and similarly, and more surprisingly, how it knows how to touch Pennsatucky's body in order to produce pain and destruction? It is because of Piper's bodily existence as both touching and touched that this kind of reciprocity can emerge. In this sense, to see or touch is not to encounter an object (or another) with an isolated consciousness, but to be drawn into a world by our body's engagement with it. This experience is always one that blurs the lines between subject and object, between mind and body, and, ultimately, between self and other.

This kind of intersubjectivity is possible because the center of our being is not some private, hidden, invisible consciousness, but the openness of our bodies to the world as subject-objects that are both seeing and being seen, touching and being touched. It is the nature of our bodies to be completely at home in the world, not as just one more object among a world of objects, but as an object that is very much open to the world of other objects, touching and being touched by them. To say that my existence is incarnated is *not* to say that my "self," my "I," has been *placed into* flesh, but that my whole way of being an "I" or of having a "self" *depends upon the fleshly nature* of my existence.

Remember All Their Faces

In his last piece of writing, published posthumously as *The Visible and the Invisible*, Merleau-Ponty pushed these ideas even further. Fundamental to his approach is the idea that "consciousness" is not what sees and touches the world . . . it is my eyes, my hands, etc. that see and touch. I don't see with my consciousness; I see with my eyes. However, my eyes, lying on the table would not see; it is only my eyes, properly integrated with my body as a whole that sees.

Still, in the experience of seeing, something "invisible," something that we can describe as consciousness does seem to emerge. If Red could truly "see" what Vee was thinking, planning, intending, she could better defend herself. Though Red and Vee have similar bodies, share similar worlds, and use objects in similar ways, there's still something unseen, something invisible about Vee that Red cannot see. Vee, like the rest of us, is composed of both the visible and the invisible in ways that could tempt us to return to the mind-body opposition that Merleau-Ponty wants us to reject.

But Merleau-Ponty refuses to return to this model of the solipsistic, alienated subject. He argues that in place of a basic *opposition* of subject and objects (objects that include our own bodies and those of others), we should think of an *intertwining* of the visible and the invisible. In trying to conceptualize this intertwining he found no satisfactory philosophical concept, so he coined his own: "flesh" (*chair* in his native French). This "flesh" is more than lumps of matter or piles of organs (*Visible and Invisible*, p. 146). I touch and am touched. I see and am seen. I touch the objects I touch the way they want to be touched, and my flesh responds to this touching as flesh. The "invisible," the world of consciousness, ideas, and concepts, is possible only because this touching flesh is also the flesh that has been touched. This being touched by the world, as well as this touching of it, gives rise to all experience.

The opening credit sequence runs a series of close-ups on the eyes and mouths of actual former prison inmates, including Piper Kerman. There is a strange power in our engagement with these images. They convey emotion, and connect us to the anonymous individuals rapidly flashing across our screens. The connection we are experiencing as we view these images is not the experience of viewing objects (Sartre's view), but of viewing subjects (Merleau-Ponty's view).

According to an article in *The Huffington Post*, the title sequence, designed by Thomas Cobb Group, was created by asking former inmates to "visualize in their minds three emotive thoughts: Think of a peaceful place, think of a person who makes you laugh, and think of something you want to forget." Though we cannot have access to the details of these mental experiences, every time we watch the opening credits, looking at these eyes and mouths while hearing Regina Spektor's haunting lyrics, "Remember all their faces / Remember all their voices," the "emotive thoughts" in the minds of these women create an emotional resonance with us. This resonance, this sharing of experience, is the intertwining of the flesh described by Merleau-Ponty.

The other can see me in a way I can never see myself. Even when I look at myself in the mirror, I see only a reflection of my image and not me, myself. I cannot, as Merleau-Ponty points out, look at my own eyes. But I can look at the eyes of the other, and when I see the other I am seeing neither an object, nor a subjective gaze that turns me into an object, but I'm seeing what it is for me to see. I'm looking at the same kind of looking that I employ when I'm the one looking. What gives the opening sequence of the show its particularly powerful emotional "feel" is that we are not looking at "objects" on the screen, nor are we being looked at by a gaze that converts us into an object; we are looking at the human experience of life—emotion expressed in flesh, flesh like our own—and our response is an experience of shared subjectivity.

The brilliant actors who comprise the cast of *Orange Is the New Black embody* the characters they play. Their portrayals are not a trick, an illusion, or a deception. They bring the characters to life with their bodies, with their faces, and with their voices as incarnated subjects sharing experience with other incarnated subjects, namely, the viewers.

This transaction makes it clear to us that as we engage with others we are certainly capable of viewing them as objects and treating them accordingly, but to do so is to deny the very nature of what our nature is, namely, an incarnated, intersubjective, openness to the world. It is in this openness that our flesh touches, and is touched by this world, which is this openness, and that touched and touching flesh is who we are.[1]

---

[1] Special thanks to Corinne Hoelscher for sharing *Orange Is the New Black* with me and for reading a draft of this chapter.

VII

My brain will always be there for you

13
The Chicken and the Egg-sistential Crisis

Leigh Duffy

Try to look at your experience here as a mandala, Chapman. Work hard to make something as meaningful and beautiful as you can. And when you're done, pack it in and know it was all temporary.

Yoga Jones sagely offers this advice to Piper Chapman during their first real conversation in the pilot episode of *Orange Is the New Black*. Yet, as we soon learn, it's impossible for anyone at Litchfield penitentiary to create anything meaningful or beautiful.

Some of the inmates seem genuinely concerned with finding meaning and beauty as they serve their time, so my argument is not that these women aren't trying or that there's something wrong with *them*. Instead, there is something about life within the prison walls that takes away from the very meaningfulness of their acts. In fact, the only way to live a meaningful life behind bars is for the prisoners to change the very conditions under which they are confined.

A Meaningful Life

Susan Wolf's theory on the meaningfulness of life captures much of our intuitions about meaningfulness.

Wolf says that a meaningful life is one in which subjective attraction meets objective attractiveness. When asked for examples of people who *clearly* lived a meaningful life, many people will name Gandhi, Mother Teresa, Jesus, or Martin Luther King Jr. Dr. King's life meets Wolf's conditions because he had the subjective attraction: he was actively engaged with and gripped by his work. His work was also objectively attractive: working for civil rights is *good*.

For Wolf, what counts and what does not count as an objectively worthwhile project requires us to use our judgment, and then there's a lot of gray area in between. An obsessive rubber band collector, for example, is engaged or gripped by her activity, but she is not engaged in a worthwhile activity because collecting rubber bands is, we tend to feel, not a meaningful way to spend our time. Similarly, if Litchfield Corrections Officer, Sam Healy's life is meaningful at all, it would not be due to his plastic bobble head collection since that too would be a trivial way to spend one's time.

The project must also be in some sense *good*. Hitler's life certainly had an impact on others and changed the course of history, but living a historically important life is not the same as living a meaningful life. According to Wolf's conditions, Hitler's life was not meaningful. In a similar way, Vee's life was not meaningful either. She was clearly actively engaged in all of her actions while at Litchfield, but none of her actions were *good*.

On the other hand, a physician in West Africa working with ebola patients through Doctors Without Borders is spending her time in a non-trivial and good way. If she's also passionate about her work, then her work gives her life meaning. If, however, she is uninterested in the work, but she is there seeking to be praised or because her parents forced her into medicine, then she would be lacking the subjective attraction and hence this particular activity would not make her life meaningful. Similarly, Sister Ingalls may have been involved in a worthwhile activity of protesting the production of nuclear weapons and she may have been passionately involved in that protest. However, if she was not passionate about the activism but rather about fame, her passion would be misdirected and so this act itself would not be what gives her life meaning.

Many of the women at Litchfield do meet these conditions and yet they still fall short of living a meaningful life. Again, this is not to show something that's wrong with the women, nor is it to argue against Wolf's theory. Rather it shows that something is wrong with the conditions under which they are supposed to live meaningfully. None currently have lives that we would identify as meaningful. Even when the requirements are met, there's something lacking. Litchfield is failing in any attempt to help these women better their lives. And if Litchfield is a reflection of our actual penal system, we have reason to worry.

Red

Red's got passion, that's for sure. We see it with her extreme reaction to Piper's foolish comment about how awful the food is and with her reaction to being forced out of the kitchen. When she's told that, "Betty died," the audience assumes by her reaction that Betty is one of the older white women inmates. Red is so engaged with her kitchen that she takes the loss of the refrigerator personally.

When Red loses her core group of friends after trying to sabotage Mendoza's position as chef, she's devastated. She's passionately involved with her "family." Her disappointment in Nicky when she suspects her of taking drugs is the disappointment of a concerned mother who is actively engaged in her daughter's well-being. In flashbacks, we see Red mothering Nicky through her detox and the picture of this relationship becomes clear. Red has become the mother Nicky never had and always needed.

Red's passion is directed at worthwhile endeavors. Cooking for and, more generally, being a caretaker of, others are clearly worthwhile ways to spend her time. Still, Red is constantly frustrated in her attempts to be engaged in her activities. There's no money to get proper ingredients or appliances and she even has to fool Healy into replacing "Betty."

Red faces constant struggles in her efforts to create something beautiful in her kitchen and in her life. She can't get proper ingredients or equipment. Pornstache antagonizes her and interferes with her cooking, like when he pees in the Thanksgiving gravy. All of her efforts to maintain her family are upended when Vee returns. Vee and the guards pose huge obstacles to her being able to do her job *well*. The freedom she may have been able to enjoy outside of the prison walls—freedom that would allow her create something beautiful—is taken away and she can no longer create something meaningful.

Poussey

Poussey is also actively engaged in meaningful projects in her relationships with others. If you didn't know better, you'd assume that Poussey's and Taystee's friendship was born years ago, as children. They are that close and comfortable with each other. Even when Poussey realized that this relationship would never evolve into something romantic, she stayed by Taystee's side because she'd rather have her simply as a friend than not at all, although it is clear that she loves Taystee.

When interviewed about the nature of "love," Poussey says, "It's just chillin', you know? Kicking it with somebody, talking, making mad stupid jokes. And like, not even wanting to go to sleep 'cause then you might be without them for a minute. And you don't want that." This is exactly what we see with Taystee and Poussey very early on in the show: Taystee and Poussey joking, pretending to be upper-class white women, laughing.

Still, when Taystee's up for parole, Poussey actively helps her gain her freedom. She's doing what's best for her friend because she is actively engaged with the friendship, wanting to do what's right and what's best. That kind of relationship is surely one that is a worthwhile endeavor. The worthiness of Poussey's actions extend beyond simply being a friend to Taystee. Poussey also seems concerned with doing the right thing in a more general sense. Although it might not seem like making toilet hooch is *good*, you could argue the worthiness of this project as she's doing it *for* others. Poussey brings Tricia's friends the hooch to help them as they're mourning her death. Poussey's interest in giving these women the hooch is not selfish. Unlike Vee, whose interest in bringing in cigarettes and drugs is purely selfish, Poussey wants to do something to *help* Tricia's friends in their time of sorrow.

Yet Poussey and Taystee are constantly frustrated in their efforts to make something meaningful or beautiful of their experience at Litchfield as well. Vee underhandedly works to destroy their friendship. She gets Poussey taken out of the library and then works to turn Taystee and her other friends against her. Vee's passive-aggressive comments to Taystee plant the seed that turns Taystee against her friend. That could have happened outside the prison walls, but what's troubling here is that the prison guards are not going to help Poussey do right either. No one is punished after Vee has Crazy Eyes attack a drunk Poussey in the bathroom. No one even questions Poussey's claims that she simply fell down. Her attempts to do something meaningful and *good* are overlooked. They ignore the big issues of mistreatment because they don't want to deal with yet another problem.

The general way of life in prison frustrates Poussey's attempts at doing something meaningful while at Litchfield. Doing good is not encouraged. The guards would rather reward snitches or ignore the big problems because they know those are unsolvable. It might seem as if Poussey has the choice to do right, but there is no genuine choice here when you consider the consequences of those actions. The guards here want to do the bare minimum to keep things quiet. In fact, that's basically what Healy says when he asks Piper to run for WAC (the Women's Advisory Council). He tells her that with her help, they could make this place a little quieter—not better, not fair, not more just, but *quiet*.

Taystee

Taystee is actively engaged in the library. In one scene, she tells another inmate not to use *Harry Potter* as a stepstool, but rather to use *Ulysses*. She says that although everyone calls it "genius," she calls it "bullshit." ("Ain't nobody got time for that!") Even though she doesn't appreciate *Ulysses*, it seems she's at least read it and has an opinion about it. She shows passion for literature. She's got thoughts on which books are worth reading.

Taystee's ability to maintain an active engagement with this *particular* worthwhile activity—reading—isn't what worries me though. It's her more general efforts to *better* herself, through reading or otherwise. Not only is Taystee obviously interested in literature, but, in flashbacks, we see Taystee as mature, intelligent, funny, charming, and something of an entrepreneurial spirit. Later, we see her as having potential in the outside world when she shows her skill at the mock job fair. Taystee impresses the judge with her research of the company and nails the interview.

The powers that be at Litchfield give Taystee a chance to live a meaningful life *outside* the prison walls. She receives her appeal and we have good reason to believe she *could* do something meaningful once she's released. However, Taystee has nowhere to go, no one to turn to, and nothing to do once she's out. She doesn't know how to live. She's mentioned that she's been in "institutions" all her life and these institutions have done her no favors in preparing her to live in the real world, let alone to live *meaningfully!* Taystee ends up right back in Litchfield.

Alex

Something similar happens to Alex Vause. When she's released after testifying against Kubra, Alex cannot live meaningfully back in her tiny Queens apartment. Not only is she unhappy in her current situation, she's unable to function as she's in constant fear that someone from her former life as a drug importer is coming to harm her or kill her. The system is doing nothing substantial to protect either her life or her mental health.

Taystee and Alex face similar obstacles. The system itself stands in their way of doing anything meaningful inside or outside of the prison walls. In this case, the system that was supposed to rehabilitate them and give them a second chance has failed. Not only can they not find a way to live meaningfully *inside* the prison (all Taystee's work in the mock interview was for nothing; there was no promise of a real job at the end), but their ability to do something worthwhile outside of the prison is also severely affected by the lack of support they've received from the system itself. The most severe case of this is Jimmy, one of the goldens, who's released with nowhere to go and no one to turn to, even though everyone knows full well that she's not mentally or physically healthy enough to survive on her own.

The Animals, the Animals

Many of the other women at Litchfield are engaged with projects or activities that are meaningful or beautiful in their own ways. For example, spending time on relationships, even the most difficult ones, is a worthy way to spend one's time. In fact, Susan Wolf is clear about the fact that many worthwhile activities will cause a certain amount of grief, pain, and suffering when we're actively engaged with them.

Red, Gina, and Norma; Flaca and Ramos; Sophia and Sister Ingalls; Mercy and Tricia (and formerly Mercy and Big Boo); Nicky and Lorna; Taystee and Poussey; Piper and Alex; Alex and Nicky—these relationships involve a certain amount of attraction, passion, and engagement, whether that attraction is physical or something more platonic and many strike the viewer as meaningful. For example, Sister Ingalls seems selflessly motivated to help Sophia. The Sister becomes an ear for Sophia and tries to help her make peace with her past and to move forward with her son.

We see active engagement in other activities: Watson is engaged with running; Yoga Jones is engaged with yoga; some of the "goldens" are engaged with knitting (and one of them gets so "in the zone" that she won't respond to Piper when she tries to strike up a conversation in the cafeteria). These women try to create something beautiful; there is the beauty of a well-cooked and well-presented meal, the beauty in love, and the beauty in true friendship, the beauty of self-improvement. Many of these women meet Wolf's requirements, so why don't these lives *strike us* as meaningful? What's missing from the lives of the inmates that make it feel like they are not worthwhile?

Part of the problem is financial: programs get cut, groups lose their space, tracks close, ingredients are limited, bathrooms can't be repaired. But the bigger problem is that the women here are being treated in such a way that they're encouraged *not* to make something meaningful of their lives or even of their time in prison. The worry is not that the guards, officers, and wardens are not encouraging them or helping them find meaning. It's bigger than that. The worry is that the guards, officers, and wardens are actively working to keep these women from doing anything meaningful. Running, knitting, reading, cooking: none of these activities are given to help these women do something meaningful or beautiful with their time. Rather, they are distractions from the reality of their lives at Litchfield. Rather than give these women genuine choices to fulfill their own subjective attraction toward worthwhile activities, they give them an illusion of choice and of meaning.

It seems though that there might be two instances of characters who are actively engaged in projects of worth that *do* give meaning to their experience in prison. But it is only because these two examples are engaged in projects that are actively trying to *change* the very conditions of the prison system to which they are subject that these can be considered instances of meaningfulness or value.

Piper

The first is Piper. Consider Piper's life when she first arrives at Litchfield. She tries to stay focused on her business so that she doesn't "lose it" while in prison. But her business is making *artisanal bath products*. When compared to running for a position on the Women's Advisory Council on the platform of universal health care and human rights (which Sophia does), Piper's "business" sounds extremely trivial and not a worthy endeavor at all.

Piper tries to find other activities in which to be engaged; she runs, she reads, she makes friends (against Healy's advice), she does yoga, she attempts to write appeals for some of the other inmates. But all of these activities face their own obstacles. She's passionately engaged in some and not at all in others, but in any case, she cannot be successful in any of them due to the constraints she faces as a prisoner.

What does give Piper's life some meaning is when she starts the prison newsletter. She gets the other women to be actively engaged in spreading their ideas and passions. That's important, for sure. But more importantly, this is a front to help a reporter break a story about the misallocation of prison money. Piper's actions in this case become meaningful because she's working to change the very conditions under which these women have to find a way to live meaningfully. Piper's fake newsletter is all an effort to make changes at Litchfield.

Soso

The second example, ironically enough, is Soso. Like Sister Ingalls, Soso is an activist but she seems to have less selfish motivation. That's not to ignore her annoying self-*involvement*, but her interest in staging a hunger strike is not for fame but to change the conditions of the prison. Her refusal to shower too is not to gain any friends—in fact people are repulsed by her and by this act—but to make a statement about the unfairness of having this personal *choice* taken away. When Wanda forces her into the shower, Soso collapses to the floor in a show of "passive resistance."

Soso's experience here might also be thwarted by the very conditions of the prison—she is eventually forced to shower and to eat—but it seems that her efforts are more meaningful than anything the other women are involved in simply *because* she's trying to change the conditions for them all. She's trying to rid them of the obstacles they all face living at Litchfield. If she were able to do that, these other women might be able to participate in meaningful activities after all.

The Chicken

In one of the greatest episodes of the first season, "The Chickening," Piper sees a chicken in the prison yard and all the women at Litchfield become obsessed with trying to catch the chicken. Piper's certain the chicken is real. Nicky wonders whether she really saw a spruce goose. Red believes it is not just any chicken, but *the* chicken that came to her in a dream. Her family searches because Red wants "to eat a chicken, smarter than all other chickens, and absorb its powers." The Spanish "tribe" starts to hunt for the chicken because they suspect it might have thousands of dollars' worth of drugs inside it. The other women at Litchfield hear of this and soon everyone is on this crazy chicken hunt, running like mad around the prison yard.

After things calm down, Healy reprimands Piper, having her repeat after him, "There is no chicken" and as she leaves his office, we hear Wanda over the PA system, "The chicken is an urban myth. A grand illusion. Something to give your life meaning, but which, is in fact, not there. We will make a poster." In the end, Piper sees the chicken again and tracks it down, but this time, she sees it outside of the prison walls. Whatever is the truth behind the chicken, the guards did *not* give the inmates a chicken in order to give their lives meaning. The announcement proclaiming that they did is in order to bring back some sense of quiet and control in the prison.

Still, those in command at Litchfield do fill the women's lives with "chickens," illusions of meaning in the prison in order to keep things a little quieter. Except for the rare exception (Taystee and Piper, respectively), nothing meaningful will come of their appeals or their requests for furlough. Though Piper and the other women in electric will not end up fixing anything, they work hard under the illusion that they might make some small change. The mock job fair too has no real value, but it gets the women under control so that Healy, Caputo, and Figueroa have less to worry about.

This is also the case with WAC, another chicken, another illusion of meaning given to the inmates. Although Piper would like to make changes to Litchfield, it is clear no one is going to work with her to do so. When Healy asks what the members of WAC want for their fellow inmates, Taystee asks for a different hot sauce—the kind from Thailand—and Maria asks for a second pillow. When it's Piper's turn, she's surprised:

"You're done?" She has bigger concerns: health care, a GED program, legal council. She claims, "We should be learning to improve ourselves as students or even as teachers."

The other inmates scoff at her, but she's right. These sorts of requests could improve the quality of life for the women at Litchfield and allow them to do something beautiful, something meaningful, in a way that hot sauce and an extra pillow would not. Healy simply turns to Chang to move on and when she has nothing to say, he says, "Good." Healy's not interested in making real changes and Taystee knows it. He just wants to make things a little quieter and by allowing the women of WAC to have the appearance of making changes, he expects to pacify the masses. It's his chicken.

Consider too how Healy defends the idea of WAC to Caputo: "This isn't about giving them power. This is about your mother telling you, you could take a bath before dinner or after. You were still gonna get wet but you thought you had a choice." He admits to giving this illusion of power while they actually have no choice. Piper can't make anything meaningful out of this project because she's still working under the powers that be and without real choice or freedom. In order to make genuine changes at Litchfield she cannot work within the conditions set *by those in power at Litchfield.*

The newsletter and her secret mission, on the other hand, are her ways to do that because those in power are not involved and these projects give her experience some meaning, some beauty. Any projects that are chickens offered to the inmates in order to give them something to do other than make waves are not real projects of worth; they are not going to give their lives meaning. But this particular project could because it is not an illusion of meaning; it is not *given* to Piper in order to keep her from stirring things up. Rather, in this case, Piper offers the newsletter as a chicken to Healy and Caputo. They see it as something over which they have control even though this project is completely in Piper's hands.

Release

Jones tells Piper to think of her time here like the mandalas. The monks work for days, weeks even, to make something beautiful and then they wipe it all away. They have the right perspective because they see their work as temporary. The idea is that if Piper can make something meaningful of her experience here, when it is time to go, she can also *let it go*. But the advice is not simply to be able to let it all go, it is also to *do something*—something meaningful and beautiful—with her time here. Jones truly has adopted the yogic perspective. The yoga approach is to cultivate non-attachments to the outcomes of our actions and still, with the time we have here, to do our dharma, our selfless, noble duty. Time spent in Litchfield, as time spent on Earth, is best spent by doing something positive and for others.

Red, Poussey, Taystee, Piper, and Soso might all be trying to do just that. Still, there's a difference between them and the mandala-making monks. The monks not only *choose* to make the mandalas, they decide when they are *done*, and then the monks themselves *choose* to wipe them away. In the case of the women at Litchfield, they don't have genuine choice when it comes to their projects of worth. Healy is clear about that when he compares WAC with being a child forced into taking a bath. Nor do the inmates get a chance to finish creating something beautiful before they wipe it all away. In most cases, they're not the ones wiping it all away—

even that has been taken from them. They are not in charge of anything in their lives, not even the projects that are supposed to give them meaning or merely an illusion of meaning! Before they get to finish their mandalas, Pornstache, Healy, or Fig are there to wipe it all away.

Jones also says that you have to recognize that the meaningful and beautiful are all temporary. However, she does not give this as advice in order to live *meaningfully*. Rather her advice is to help Piper *survive*. Jones says "Survival here is all about perspective." These women are frustrated in their attempts because of the guards and those in charge, but they *suffer* because of their perspective. They might be in Litchfield for a *long* time, but to recognize this experience as temporary is to be able to survive without suffering.

Wolf's idea that we have to be passionately involved in acts in order for them to be meaningful is directly opposed to this yogic view. According to Wolf the result of active engagement is often some sense of pain or suffering. For Jones, becoming disengaged or non-attached will release suffering and grant an ability to survive under these conditions.

I believe in the yogic approach when the desired result it to decrease suffering. Still, I don't think it's enough to find a way for these women at Litchfield, or for inmates in actual prisons, to simply not suffer. Rather, we should be doing something more for them so that they are not merely "surviving" their time but finding a way to live better lives. This is nothing new. There is a long-standing debate about what role prison is to play and whether the goal here is to punish or to rehabilitate. What I want to add to that question is the consideration of how the people in charge might also be affected.

Consider the lives of the guards and the wardens or others in charge and how their lives might become meaningful. If they are actively involved in their jobs and in running a prison system, then in order for that to give their lives meaning, that project itself must be somehow positive and good. In order for it to count as dharma in the yogic sense, it must be selfless.

If the people in charge are only working to punish these women, or in order to simply maintain some sense of order or quiet, we cannot consider this a meaningful experience or a meaningful way to use their time. If, however, these people in charge are engaged in helping the inmates better themselves or find meaning or do something beautiful and positive, then those in charge could themselves live a meaningful life. Not only is it their duty to the inmates to help them become better, it is a way for people like Healy, Caputo, and Fig to find meaning themselves, and to make their lives worth living. Even if Jones is right and we need to look at our time here as temporary, we do have an obligation to do something beautiful and meaningful while we are here and that means that those with power, at Litchfield or otherwise, seem to have a further obligation to help those without power do something meaningful as well.[1]

[1] Thanks to Hillary Reeves and Tom Wall who both read drafts of this chapter and got me to think more carefully about the meaning of my own argument. And thanks to Kimberly Blessing who got me to think about meaning in the first place!

14
What Friends Are For

CHARLENE ELSBY AND ROB LUZECKY

Red originates as a person of immense power, whose whims decide if a prisoner is allowed to eat or not to eat. This power stems from her position as head of the kitchen, a position she maintains by having many friends. These friends are gained through her usefulness, as a purveyor of rare goods, like pantyhose and lipstick.

Aristotle maintains that a friendship of utility—someone who's a friend only because you're useful to them—is really no kind of friendship at all. Although a real friend is also useful, utility alone cannot be the basis of true friendship.

Friendship of utility is the kind of friendship most noticeable in Litchfield, where it seems that real friendship is almost impossible. In a context where things we take for granted are rarities, friendships of utility are of the utmost importance, and it is through these kinds of friendships that you can get to a higher rung on the social hierarchy. Red's rise, fall, and comeback as a power figure in Litchfield shows how she strives to maintain a delicate balance of social alliances, utility, and power.

What's a Friend?

The word "friend" is used in many ways. In normal conversation, we might use the word "friend" to refer to someone we often meet socially. A friend is a person whose company we enjoy, with whom we engage in enjoyable activities; a friend is someone whose qualities we appreciate, someone whose existence in some way complements our own.

We relate to our friends; a friendship is something valuable for its own sake. When we envision someone as a friend, we like to think we are not *using* this person. But what does that mean? A friend is someone with whom we associate ourselves not merely for what they can do for us, but is something better than that. If we didn't, we might say, "Oh, she's not a friend. I'm just using her for her employee discount." The concepts of using someone, and their being a friend, might even be mutually exclusive.

Defined in such a way, Red does not have many friends at all. Red's friends are not there to enjoy her quick wit or life experience. They take no joy in her simply as a person. Red is only valuable as someone who can *provide*. She's not really a friend, but someone with whom these women are *friendly*. What does it mean to be friendly? Well, we might say that the adjective refers to someone having the quality of a friend, but in this case, it's more likely that they have the quality of being *like* a friend. Friends are people with whom we get along, it's good policy to be nice to our allies. We might envision Red as being our friend, but it would be more accurate to say that there are a lot of people who are *friendly* towards her. They act pleasantly simply because of the pay-off.

What happens when you fail to be friendly to Red? Early in the series, very bad things happen. Piper is denied food and is subject to additional punishments, merely for questioning the quality of Red's food. A friend, of course, would never do this. But Piper is not Red's friend, so why should she aspire to be friendly to Red? For purely practical reasons. The system Red has set up prior to Piper's arrival demands that everyone else submit to a demand for *friendliness.* A friend would never say such a thing; in order to be friendly, you must act as if you really are a friend; Piper did not, and will face the consequences.

Later, however, as Red's pipeline is shut down, so is her system. There is no reason anymore for the other women to be friendly to her. We might say that she has lost her friends, but this isn't really accurate. Rather, she has lost the stature that demands friendliness from the common folk.

Aristotle discusses the concept of friendship in Book VIII of the *Nicomachean Ethics.* There, he differentiates between true friendships, friendships of pleasure, and friendships of utility. True friends are defined as those who maintain a recognized, reciprocal goodwill. True friends wish the best for one another. Red's acquaintances don't seem to meet this qualification. Friendships of pleasure arise between people who find some quality in another person pleasant—their wit, for example. These friendships will last as long as does the pleasure someone can gain from them.

Friendships of utility, if they can be called friendships at all, are maintained for the sake of some good each party gets from the other. With regard to friendships of utility, Aristotle tells us that the "friendship" part of the friendship is really only incidental—it is not the friend that is loved, but the benefit you get from them. It is entirely possible to have a friendship of utility with someone you don't even find pleasant.

For obvious reasons, these friendships easily dissolve when the benefit is no longer available.

We see this theory enacted through Red. One of the goods she has to offer, while in charge of the kitchen, is really just being free from the horrible things that could happen to you were you to piss off the woman in charge of the kitchen. The other goods she has to offer are actual goods—maintaining friendly relations with Red means you can take advantage of the Neptune's Produce pipeline.

At the end of Season One, the kitchen is taken away from her, and along with it, her utility to the other inmates. Red's so-called friends no longer have any reason to associate with her, while those who might be called actual friends seem to have something against the fact that her botched attempt at kitchen sabotage leads to one of her own being severely burned.

A Friend "In Here" versus "Out There"?

Another common conception of friendship to which Aristotle refers in the *Nicomachean Ethics* is the idea that like attracts like—your friends are more likely similar to you than dissimilar. It's easy to say that opposites attract, sure, but it's just less likely that you'll be friends with someone entirely dissimilar to yourself. The people with whom you associate are limited by the places you frequent, and the chances you'll run into them. The people who really are our opposites are probably people we'll never even meet.

You would think that in Litchfield, it could go one of two ways: either you'll end up being friends with people who are similar to you, or you'll be forced to interact with people with whom you'd never interact with otherwise (like how Pennsatucky ends up making friends with Big Boo). In different ways, both of these end up happening.

One of the first things Piper learns when she gets into Litchfield is that who her friends will be has already been decided. There's a division between races that determines with whom she'll be spending her time. In having pissed off Red, Piper has pissed off the whole white race (at least, its representatives in Litchfield). We don't normally decide who our friends are based on skin color (at least, I hope not), but in Litchfield your default friends are those who share your race. It's not as if there's no conflict among people of one's own race; Piper and Pennsatucky's showdown is enough to show that's false. But with regard to the larger system, unity is maintained against members of other racial groups in competitions for the best jobs and movie seats. We might question how likely it is that you'll share similar characteristics with people of your own race as opposed to others. We might have more in common with people of similar position, socioeconomic status, or a mutual interest in yoga. But that's how the system works here. Red's posse is a diverse bunch of incarcerated women united by skin color.

Just like when Piper pisses of Red, and she is ostracized, when Red's kitchen sabotage leads to disastrous results, she's out on her own. At this point she happens into another group, with another seemingly accidental quality in common—the old people. The old women, who, they say, nobody notices anymore, band together; being old supersedes the race qualification. Perhaps if Red weren't old enough to have white roots she wouldn't have found another group and would have never regained power. But she is, and she did. She used those old women to work in her greenhouse, the new pipeline system, to play the old game a new way.

When Vee enters the prison, we see her set up a system that parallels Red's. These two women have old business to take care of, similar ways of dealing with the people around them, and similar kinds of friendship. If it weren't for the brutal competition between them, they might even have become true friends.

Red and Vee

In a certain sense, Vee and Red's characters mirror each other. Red, with her "fierce" hair and Vee, with her imperious look, both cut imposing figures. They seem to have a type of friendship that while not exactly genuine, seems to be more than merely a friendship of utility.

Recall when we're first introduced to the character of Vee in Season Two's "Looks Blue, Tastes Red." She's sitting on a park bench at the Black Adoption Festival. A young RJ comes up to her and presents her with the proceeds from some recent drug deals. Vee weighs the roll of bills in her hand and questions RJ about whether or not he has skimmed some of the money. Along with this questioning, there is the explicit threat: "light is not right, unless you like sleeping on the street." If RJ took any money from Vee's profits, he'll be homeless. Vee is the matriarch of her "family," and she rules with an iron fist.

We see Vee's cold-heartedness again in "What Is the Change," when Vee sleeps with RJ and has him killed. First a few moments of intimacy, then an assassination, and then—presumably—a few tears at the funeral; it's difficult to see Vee as anything other than a person who is motivated by the desire for self-preservation, and it seems that she is completely incapable of forming any deep human connection. In this sense, she is a sort of monster, who identifies those who are vulnerable (like

Crazy Eyes, when she is still afraid of "Dandelion") and bolsters their courage only if those people can serve her purposes. (In a fight, Crazy Eyes makes some great muscle. Just ask Piper). Finally, look at how Vee turns her back on Taystee. "Friendship" seems to be a foreign concept to Vee, and she only tries to befriend people to build-up an army of sorts. If we look at Vee's character, it is difficult to conceive of her as a friend in any sense of the word, but she most certainly reveals herself to be an enemy to be feared.

Similarly, Red is no one to mess with. While she may express some remorse for what happened to Gina in "Can't Fix Crazy," Red knew that sabotaging the kitchen might very well involve inflicting pain on another person. Red demonstrates that when she is backed in to corner, she will act, and she will act decisively, regardless of whether or not someone might get hurt. This might make Red seem a very unlikable character, flawed in the sense that she lacks any sense of morality and any capacity to form meaningful friendships. But then we see Red expressing concern about her son's black eye when he comes to visit her. She also is genuinely concerned about the well-being of her store (and her family) in "The Little Mustachioed Shit." Yes, Red is not someone to be trifled with, but this is perhaps because she cares about the things and people close to her, and does not want to see them suffering. With these personality traits in mind, Red seems like the best friend that one could have, and the worst person that one could ever cross.

When Vee and Red meet (again) in "Hugs Can Be Deceiving," it's like seeing two seasoned warriors sizing each other up. They trade verbal barbs, they trade observations about the present pecking order at Litchfield, and they never break eye contact. They talk about the glories of past victories, and the ignominy of recent defeats. Each seems to know what the other is capable of. Each seems to know what the other can do. You get the sense that each carries on the conversation looking for the upper-hand. Vee feigns a truce between her and Red when she says that she is "just going to read some books, keep her head down, and do her time, just as the good Lord intended," but neither she nor Red takes this as a true statement of her intent. Everybody knows that, sooner or later, these two will cross each other. Their hug is indeed deceiving, for they are two beings with nearly identical characters, each competing for a position of power in the prison hierarchy.

Through the course of the season, both Vee and Red build up their respective forces. Red's observation that nothing has changed reveals itself to be true. Red starts building relationships by providing rare goods to the other inmates. Vee starts building relationships by providing drugs to the inmates. It might seem that both characters are identical save for the fact that they are in opposition, but this would not be entirely accurate.

Although Vee and Red are similar in their aims to control the flow of contraband into Litchfield, both seem to have radically different motives. In addition to supplying rare goods, Red safeguards Nicky from re-lapsing into drug addiction. While Red's actions aren't exactly the selfless actions of a saint, they do indicate that she has some sort of relationship with Nicky that extends beyond that of mere utility. (Nicky would have still consumed the rare goods that Red provided, re-gardless of whether or not she was using heroin). That is, she is showing genuine concern for Nicky's well-being. In helping to prevent Nicky's relapse, Red shows that she actually cares for someone other than herself;

she is capable of treating people as something more than simply pawns to be used. Red shows that underneath her fierce exterior, despite the seeming impossibility of forming genuine bonds of friendship in a place like Litchfield, she can exhibit the caring of a genuine friend. In this example, Red shows that she wishes good for Nicky, for Nicky's own sake, so here is true friendship in Aristotle's definition.

Red versus Vee—Friendship and Respect

To understand the nature of genuine friendship, we need to point out that sometimes caring is not enough. Simply caring for a person does not guarantee that they will be your friend; we can care about a lot of things that don't care back at us. But what does it mean to like someone, anyway? Perhaps we can substitute the word "like" for "respect." If you respect someone, you appreciate their qualities, not for what they bring you, but for their own sake. That sounds like friendship to us.

Ideally, in order to be someone's friend, not only must you respect them, this respect must be reciprocated. If there is both respect and caring involved in the relationship, then that relationship is one of genuine friendship. But while respect seems like part of a good friendship, it's possible, as Red and Vee show us, to respect someone and also try to kill them (something we like to think our friends would not do). To respect someone doesn't mean that you care about their wellbeing. Perhaps it's just a matter of recognizing in someone else a quality you admire. In any case, it seems natural that true friends should respect one another, while not at all true that any two people who respect each other are true friends. This is how Red and Vee maintain some kind of relation, of a sort that mimics friendship, while not being so.

To understand the role respect plays in a genuine friendship, let's look at Red's attempt to kill Vee and its aftermath. It's clear enough that Red didn't particularly care about Vee when she tried to kill her. Philosophers tend to define caring for someone as the desire to not bring harm to them. (And this is the opposite of what friends wish for each other, which is only good.) It would be very strange to think that Red cares for Vee and that she demonstrates this care by trying to strangle her with a piece of plastic wrap. However, this lack of caring for Vee does not translate into a lack of respect. Respect involves recognizing that something poses a threat, that something can harm you, and treating it with extreme caution. We respect those things that have power either equal to or greater than ours. (None of the inmates had any respect for Pornstache in Season Two, because he was removed from the prison and had no power to harm them in any way). Red certainly knew that Vee could harm her, and while she certainly didn't care about Vee (she had no interest in preserving Vee's well- being), she certainly knew that she was a threat, and because of this knowledge Red respected Vee.

Perhaps this makes respect seem to be identical with fear, insofar as both involve a genuine concern for your well-being. The difference between the two is that fear seems to be a bit more resolute than respect. When we fear something, we tend to not allow for any possibility that the thing can change. When we fear something, we want to avoid it at all costs, or, if we're forced to confront it, we want to eliminate it.

When Red approached Vee from behind in the rainy night, that fear was not what she felt. There was nothing stopping her from snuffing out Vee's life; Vee was on her back, down on the ground, but something stopped Red from tightening her grip, there was a little sliver of hope that Vee might be worth saving, and this sliver was respect for Vee. Whatever the crimes Vee had committed in the past, whatever threats she had made against Red, whatever her capacities for violence and cold-heartedness, for Red, Vee was not simply an object to be feared. When Red saw those flickers of life in Vee's eyes, she saw something, something that made life worthwhile; she saw something worth respecting, and she let Vee go. Of course this didn't stop Vee. The respect Red had for Vee was only reciprocated by a weighted sock to the back of Red's head and a broken eye socket.

Red's propensity for caring is the only thing that could have stopped her from killing Vee when she had the chance. While she may not care for Vee herself, she saw in Vee a quality she respects. If it's possible to respect Vee, then perhaps it's possible to care about her. If Red doesn't care herself, perhaps someone else will. That's what makes Vee worth saving—some recognition that there is a quality there worth respect.

This recognition, by Red, is what distinguishes her from Vee, her evil counterpart. Red has the capacity to care, while for Vee, the capacity to care is just a thing in other people, another thing to be used. While both women develop powerful positions by using other people, Vee is incapable of forming true friends. And according to Aristotle, no one would choose to live that way. We might as well run them over with a van.

15
The Litchfield Prisoner's Dilemma

RICHARD GREENE

You find yourself incarcerated in Litchfield Correctional Institution, and are offered the opportunity to have your sentence reduced substantially or to possibly even gain your immediate release? Of course you would take it, right?

Not so fast. It depends a lot on what's waiting for you on the outside.

This is exactly the situation Piper Chapman finds herself in at the beginning of Season Two of *Orange Is the New Black*. She also finds herself in a close variation on the Traditional Prisoner's Dilemma.

The Traditional Prisoner's Dilemma

The Prisoner's Dilemma is a thought experiment employed by many scholars, including philosophers, mathematicians, and economists. Here's how it works.

Suppose that Tiffany "Pennsatucky" Doggett and Yvonne "Vee" Parker (a couple of Litchfield's more deplorable and ruthless inmates) are arrested for selling meth to local kids, and are being interrogated by the police. Just to make things a bit more fun, suppose that

Pennsatucky is being interrogated by George "Porn-stache" Mendez, and Vee is being interrogated by Na-talie Figueroa (Pornstache is far and away Litchfield's most unethical corrections officer—not to mention being television's "douchiest" character ever, and Figueroa is the self-serving and highly corrupt Execu-tive Assistant to the Warden at Litchfield).

Suppose that Pennsatucky is in one interrogation room and Vee is in another. Suppose further that Figueroa and Pornstache don't have enough evidence to convict either on the charge of distributing metham-phetamines to minors (I'm not a lawyer and have no idea whether distributing methamphetamines to mi-nors is a real law, but since this is just an example, I'll trust you, dear reader, to afford me a bit of latitude), but they do have enough evidence to convict both Vee and Pennsatucky on lesser, but still serious charges, perhaps, possession of a Class 1 narcotic (I think I sounded more convincing this time!).

Both Pennsatucky and Vee are made the following offer. If you testify against your partner, and your part-ner does not testify against you, then you will go free, and your partner will get a sentence of fifteen years to life. If you testify against your partner and your part-ner also testifies against you, then you will each get seven years. If neither testifies against the other (in other words, if both accomplices remain silent), then each will likely be convicted of the lesser offense and get a one year sentence. Since Vee and Pennsatucky are in separate rooms, neither knows what the other is going to do. So, what should they do?

Of course, the best thing from Vee's perspective is to testify and have Pennsatucky remain silent. Under these circumstances, Vee would go free. Similarly, the best thing from Pennsatucky's perspective is to testify against Vee and have Vee remain silent, which would mean that Pennsatucky would go free. Unfortunately, for Vee and Pennsatucky, if each goes for the optimal strategy—the one where they get no jail time—and testifies against the other, then they both get seven years. Notice that they would each be better off if neither testified against the other. Under this scenario, they would each just get one year. So, at this point it appears that the ideal thing to happen (ideal looking at it from their point of view) is for each to remain silent and not testify. Again, it is better to take the one year, than to go for no years, and end up with seven years.

Things are also complicated by the fact that no matter what the other one does each is better off if they testify. So no matter what Vee does, Pennsatucky is better off if she testifies against Vee (and vice versa). Consider the case where Vee stays silent. Under this circumstance Pennsatucky can either stay silent or testify. If Pennsatucky stays silent, she gets one year. If Pennsatucky testifies, then she will go free. It is in her interest to testify, if Vee Stays silent.

What about the case in which Vee testifies against Pennsatucky? Under this circumstance, Pennsatucky can either also testify or remain silent. If she testifies, then she gets four years. If she remains silent, then she gets fifteen years to life. So if Vee testifies, then it is in Pennsatucky's best interest to also testify.

So we have a classic dilemma argument. If Vee deoes not testify, then Pennsatucky should testify. If Vee does testify, Pennsatucky, should testify. Therefore, either way, the rational thing for Pennsatucky to do is to testify. The same is true for Vee. But as we've seen if both do the rational thing, then both are worse off (it's better for both to remain silent, than for both to testify).

It's important to the thought experiment, that both Vee and Pennsatucky are sort of despicable, as neither can count on the other to do anything but act in her own best interest. (For that matter, it helps the example to have Pornstache and Figueroa making the offers. Both are lacking in moral fortitude, so to speak. Perhaps more ethical jailors would have simply leveled with their prisoners, informing them that they have enough evidence to convict them of the lesser charges, and subsequently seeking to pursue the lesser charges.)

If both Vee and Pennsatucky are aware that the other will know that they are always better off testifying, and that each is looking out for number one, it becomes very tough for either to do the thing that makes the most sense for the two of them—remain silent, which is why the Prisoner's Dilemma is a true paradox: each person doing the rational thing (at least from a self-interested point of view) results in everyone being worse off than if they had not done the rational thing, which ironically renders the rational thing to do the irrational thing.

The Seductive Alex Vause

Prisoner's Dilemmas come in a variety of forms, and have innumerable variations. What they all have in common is the feature described above: each person doing the rational thing yields the result that each is worse off than they would be if they had done the thing that is best for the group. In the episode "Thirsty Bird" the protagonist of *Orange Is the New Black*, Piper Chapman, finds herself in one of these variant prisoner dilemmas.

Here's the set-up. Piper is imprisoned for the role she played ten years earlier (she was twenty-two years old at the time) in an international drug smuggling operation. Piper was somewhat naïve, and was mostly just doing what her lesbian lover, Alex Vause, was telling her to do. Piper had carried a bag of drug money through Customs; she was ultimately indicted on the basis of this. Fast forward to current times, where Piper finds herself incarcerated alongside Alex, who still appears to wield quite a bit of power over Piper, due in no small part to the fact that Piper still has strong amorous feelings for Alex.

Early in her time in Litchfield, Piper had been continually harassed and bullied by Pennsatucky. Things eventually came to a head, and Piper realized that the only way to stop the harassment is to fight Pennsatucky, whom Piper beat severely (watching this was perhaps the most satisfying moment of the series). Piper was placed in the SHU (the "Secure Housing Unit" or solitary confinement). While in the SHU Piper had no idea whether Pennsatucky survived the beating.

Season Two begins with Piper being transferred from Litchfield Correctional Institution to the Metropolitan Detention Center in Chicago. The guards responsible for transferring her are not particularly forthcoming with information, and Piper can only assume that she is being charged with Pennsatucky's murder. Soon after arriving in Chicago it becomes clear that Piper is in Chicago to testify in the trial of Kubra Balik, who is one of the heads of the drug smuggling ring she and Alex had been involved with earlier. Balik has been extradited and is up on charges. Alex is in Chicago for the same reason as Piper.

Decisions, Decisions!

Piper is initially inclined to testify against Balik. In exchange for doing so, she will be offered some leniency in her sentence. It's not initially clear how much leniency she is offered, but it is clear that the more valuable her testimony, the better it will be for her. Alex is extended a similar offer. Alex pleads with Piper to not testify against Balik. She reasons that if they testify against Balik, he will exact some form of revenge on them. Moreover, Alex has reason to believe that Balik will easily beat the charges. Furthermore, Alex informs Piper that she will not be testifying against Balik.

No matter what, Piper will take the witness stand in the trial, so not testifying essentially requires that she commit perjury, claiming that she doesn't know Balik, and that she has never met Balik. Neither Alex nor Piper are playing a huge role in the trial; they are just being used by the prosecution to establish a timeline. Whether they testify against Balik or not, will not likely affect the outcome of the trial much. This is significant because as we evaluate Piper's prisoner's dilemma, we don't have to let external considerations (such as whether a dangerous criminal will be released) overshadow our judgment of the rationality of the case.

There are some differences between Piper's case and the traditional Prisoner's Dilemma, but none of these differences are critical. For one, the exact terms of the deal Piper and Alex are offered is not known, but this difference is only superficial. It is clear, that each has something to gain from co-operating with the authorities. A second difference is that in the traditional Prisoner's Dilemma the prisoners are not allowed to have any contact with one another. In this case, Piper and Alex speak about the matter on more than one occasion and actually formulate a plan together. While this is a significant plot development in the show (an ongoing theme in *Orange Is the New Black* is that Piper loves Alex, but always winds up paying a stiff penalty for trusting her), we can suppose that Piper knows in advance from years of experience with Alex, that just because she says that she's going to do something is no guarantee that she will, in fact, do that thing.

So for all intents and purposes, when Piper is on the stand, she doesn't know what Alex will do or has already done. Finally, the deal that is offered to Alex and Piper is not an explicit "If you testify and the other one doesn't, then x happens, and if you don't testify and the other one, then y happens" situation. Still, given that the value of each one's testimony is based on whether they are the only one that is useful for helping to establish Balik's criminal timeline, one's testifying and the other one's not doing so makes the testimony of the one who helped finger Balik more valuable to the prosecution, and hence will result in more sentencing leniency.

An additional complication to this scenario stems from the fact that Piper's attorney, Mr. Bloom, (who just happens to be the father of her fiancé, Larry) advises Piper to testify against Balik. Piper explains the risk of testifying against Balik, which Mr. Bloom dismisses; although he doesn't assure Piper that the risk isn't real. He simply appeals to the principle that one must always tell the truth. Piper doesn't exactly buy this, but given her relationship with Larry, following Mr. Bloom's advice has some motivational pull for Piper.

So we can see why this is a Prisoner's Dilemma. If they both testify against Balik, then they both benefit to some extent (of course, this benefit can be offset if Balik has them killed or tortured or worse). If only one testifies, then the one who does gets a greater benefit (they were more beneficial, so they get more leniency in sentencing), and the other gets charged with perjury, which will actually make their sentence longer (they will use the testimony of the one who testified against

Balik to establish the perjury of the other). If neither testifies, then neither gets the benefit of testifying (the more lenient sentence), but neither can be shown to have perjured herself.

Again, notice that if Alex testifies, then Piper is better off if she also testifies. If Alex testifies and Piper does not, then Piper gets charged with perjury. If Alex testifies and so does Piper, then Piper gets a slightly more lenient sentence.

If Alex doesn't testify, then Piper is better off if she testifies. If Alex doesn't testify and Piper does testify, then Piper gets the most lenient sentence (again, assuming that Balik doesn't exact revenge on her). If Alex doesn't testify and neither does Piper, then neither gets anything (no lenience in sentencing and no charge of perjury).

So we have the same type of dilemma argument as before. If Alex testifies, Piper is better off if she testifies. If Alex doesn't testify, Piper is better off if she testifies. Therefore, no matter what, Piper is better off if she testifies against Balik, so reason dictates that she should testify. The same is true for Alex. The rational thing is for each to testify, but if each does the rational thing (from a self-interested point of view), then they both wind up worse off, than if they had both kept silent. If they both testify, they get just a small benefit to their sentences, and each runs the risk of being harmed by Balik or his henchmen, but if neither testify, while losing the small decrease in their sentences, neither runs the risk of Balik exacting his ugly revenge.

No Honor among Crooks or All's Fair in Love and War

Regular viewers of the show know all too well how the situation played out. Piper, following Alex's admonition, eventually decides to say on the witness stand that she never met Balik. So provided that Alex did the same thing (not finger Balik), then Alex and Piper will have done what group rationality requires, and while neither will have gotten a reduction to their sentences (which likely would have only been slight had each testified), each will have avoided Balik's revenge.

Unfortunately, Alex had a last minute change of mind. Despite the fact that she told Piper on the way to the trial that it's imperative they go into the trial united, and that they both will be safer if neither testifies against Balik, she ended up testifying against Balik, and Piper wound up worse off than when she started: she now has perjury charges to deal with, and no reduction in her original sentence.

Why did Alex change her mind? It's not entirely clear, but it may have to do with the fact that Piper told Alex (on the same van ride to the trial) that she needed to tell the truth, and that neither of them would be safe no matter what. It's not clear exactly why Piper changed her mind, either. But one compelling theory is that Piper wanted to protect Alex (who she is apparently still in love with). Moreover, she falsely believed that no harm would come from her not testifying against Balik, as Alex was almost certain to do the same. Neither of them ended up doing the right thing. Alex, it turned out, was released from prison immediately.

A Better Decision?

So what should Piper have done? Given that Alex ended up testifying against Balik, nothing that Piper could have done would have resulted in her being released from prison (that was only going to be the case if one testified and the other did not), but still testifying would have been preferable. She's facing serious perjury charges, and will likely have her sentence increased. Had she testified, she would be getting out sooner, rather than later.

But what about the threat of revenge from Balik? At this point it's just that—a threat. In cases such as these, the expected value of such threats has to be weighed against the very real consequences of more time in a very dangerous environment. Recall that in a very short time in Litchfield, Piper experienced a number of very real threats to her life and her well-being. Pennsatucky came at her with a shank, Red tried to starve her out of existence, she faced uncertain retribution for rebuking the advances of Crazy Eyes, to name a few. More prison time comes with more very real immediate threats. Moreover, were Balik to receive extensive prison time on the basis of Piper's testimony, there is some chance that none of his accomplices (recall that his operation was set-up overseas) would have any interest in harming the minor witnesses in his case. Piper should have done the rational thing.

This is where this variation of the Prisoner's Dilemma really differs from the Traditional Prisoner's Dilemma. In the traditional version, it's best if everyone doesn't do the rational thing, but in this case, there were just too many other variables. Most notably, it appears true of Alex, that regardless of her feelings for Piper, if given the opportunity to screw Piper, she will (literally and otherwise)!

Sugar and Spice and Some Things Not So Nice!

RICHARD GREENE AND
RACHEL ROBISON-GREENE

There are many reasons that *Orange Is the New Black* (both the book and the television series) is so successful: the characters are engaging, the stories are fascinating, the acting in the show is fantastic, it has a near-perfect balance of humor and drama, and, of course, as the preceding chapters illustrate, it is loaded with good philosophy (philosophy makes everything better!).

But at least part of the story of the success of *Orange Is the New Black* lies in the fact that we're obsessed with stories about women in prison. Going back to the early 1950s women-in-prison movies have been cult favorites and box office successes. (Who doesn't love John Cromwell's film noir classic *Caged*?) The same is true for women-in-prison fiction.

More recently, the covers of supermarket tabloids are a virtual chock-a-block of stories about female celebrities going to jail. Features on the likes of Lindsay Lohan, Amanda Bynes, Snooki, Lil' Kim, and Paris Hilton winding up in jail are so commonplace nowadays, news reports of these events are not even shocking (and yet still modern society eats them up like they are going out of style). The cable news network MSNBC airs documentaries about life in women's prisons almost every weekend. Yep, we love a good woman-goes-to-prison story.

Not all women-in-prison stories, however, are created equal. Just as some women-in-prison movies are masterfully crafted tales of redemption or decline or corruption, while others are vehicles for soft-core pornography, true-life stories about women in prison vary greatly as well. The stuff you tend to see in the tabloids is just sensationalist pap, but there are a number of stories about famous women in prison that tell us much about who we are as a society, our history, our darker sides, and (occasionally) our greatness.

Some of these stories involve famous women (and historical figures) who went to prison, and others involve women who became famous for going to prison (or more precisely, for the things they did that landed them in prison). Here are some of the more fascinating and noteworthy women who did time, with a brief account of what life behind bars was like for them (not every prison is a wacky as Litchfield!).

Sorry, Paris and Snooki, you didn't make the list. To get on this list you have to do more than act like a spoiled brat or drive under the influence; you've got to kill someone (or lots of people!) or bathe in the blood of slaughtered virgins, or rob banks, or piss off a reigning monarch (or the President of Russia!), or wield a pretty good ax, or, well . . . you get the idea. Piper Kerman, author of the book *Orange Is the New Black* also did not make the list, although her story is certainly fascinating (she was arrested for her role in an international drug trafficking ring!), and to all those who've seen the show but not read the book, we say: Read the book! It's different, but in its own way just as gripping. Since Piper's story has been discussed in the preceding pages of this book, we left her out of this list.

Marie Antoinette

Marie Antoinette (1755–1793) was the Queen of France during the early years of the French Revolution. She was married to King Louis XVI. The story of the French Revolution is well-known, so we won't rehearse it here, except to say that there was a peasant uprising, and the Queen was captured and sent to the Big House. She was not arrested for any particular crime, but rather, for treason against the people in her roles as a monarch in circumstances that were horrific for all French-persons, except the nobility. She was also unpopular because she was a foreigner, from Austria. Later a charge (thought by historians to be false) of sexually abusing her son was added. Also, she never said "Let them eat cake!"

Normally when someone's sent to the Big House their living conditions are not all that great: they're confined to a very small space, with no privacy, and few creature comforts. This is not true of Antoinette's first stint under arrest. She was literally sent to a big house. In 1789 she was placed under house arrest in The Tuileries Palace, one of the Royal palaces, along the banks of the River Seine in Paris. Other than being under house arrest, Antoinette's life wasn't much different than before: she attended social functions in a diplomatic capacity, she meet with whomever she liked, she had attendants, and she still wielded much political influence.

As public attitudes toward the Queen began to shift, in 1792 she was moved from the Tuileries Palace to The Temple. The Temple was a medieval fortress, in which her living arrangements more resembled a modern prison (except for all the cool medieval stuff scattered about). She remained at the Temple until her execution in 1793.

Countess Elizabeth Báthory de Ecsed

Countess Elizabeth Báthory de Ecsed (1560–1640), a.k.a. "The Blood Countess," reportedly killed over six hundred girls. Rumor has it that the Countess killed young girls in order to obtain their blood, which she would bathe in. There's no reliable evidence that she bathed in the blood of virgins, but there was overwhelming evidence that she was a ruthless serial killer. Hundreds of eyewitnesses spoke at her trial. The story about her bathing in blood is still a favorite among fans of horror (see Season Three of *Penny Dreadful*, *Diablo II*, and countless B-Horror movies from the 1950s, 1960s and 1970s). She is certainly one of Transylvania's most famous citizens, and part of the motivation for the Dracula legend.

In 1610 Countess Báthory was arrested and imprisoned in Čachtice Castle in Hungary. While she was in a castle, prison life was not opulent or comfortable. The countess was placed in solitary confinement in a room that had no windows (they had been boarded up). To make matters worse, she had to revert to bathing in water. The Countess Báthory died of unknown causes in solitary confinement in 1614.

There is a theory that the countess was the innocent victim of a political conspiracy, but that leaves a whole lot of eye-witness testimony and numerous body parts to account for.

Lizzie Borden

No need to write Lizzie Borden's (1860–1927) story, as the great nineteenth-century poet, Anonymous, has done it for us:

> Lizzie Borden took an ax
> And gave her mother forty whacks,

When she saw what she had done
She gave her father forty-one.
Yesterday in old Fall River, Mr. Andrew Borden Died
And they got his Daughter Lizzie on a charge of Homicide.
Some folks say she didn't do it, and others say of course, she did
But they all agree Miss Lizzie B. was a problem type of kid.

Well, the poem has it mostly right. It was actually Lizzie's step-mother that she killed, not her biological mother, each parent was given between ten and twenty whacks, not forty and forty-one, and the ax was more of a hatchet.

While Lizzie was acquitted of the charges (there just wasn't much by way of forensic evidence tying Lizzie to the crime, even though Lizzie was seen burning her dress just after the murders occurred), she did spend several months in jail (from August 1892 to June1893) at the Jailhouse in Taunton, Massachusetts. Her jail cell was small. It had stone walls and an iron bar door. It's not know whether she was isolated or with others. The case is still considered open, but most folks who have studied the case are convinced Lizzie did it. As to her motive, there are several theories, the most plausible elaborated by Evan Hunter (Ed McBain) in his novel *Lizzie*, that Lizzie's parents had discovered her lesbian activities.

Eleanor of Aquitaine

Typically, important female prisoners in medieval and renaissance England were not taken to a place like the Tower of London. They were often held under house arrest at a castle or a manor house.

One woman imprisoned in this way was Eleanor of Aquitaine. Eleanor played a role in the Revolt of 1173–

1174. Eleanor's sons rose up against their father, Henry II, in an attempt to replace him with his son, Henry the Younger. Eleanor assisted with troops from Aquitaine. The revolt was unsuccessful and Eleanor was held under house arrest for sixteen years at a number of different houses and castles throughout England. Her son, Richard I, freed her after the death of his father in 1189.

Another celebrated woman held under long-term house arrest was Mary Stuart (Mary, Queen of Scots).

Elizabeth Diane Frederickson Downs

In 1983 Diane Downs (born 1947), a postal worker, shot her three children with a .22 caliber handgun, killing one daughter, paralyzing her son and causing another daughter to have a stroke. She told the police that they were assaulted by a gunman on a highway in Oregon who was attempting to hijack her car, but the forensic evidence refuted her version of the story. She was charged with murder, attempted murder, and criminal assault. In 1984 she was found guilty of all three charges. Her oldest daughter testified in the trial that it was, in fact, Downs who did the shooting. Police suspected that the motive for the shootings was that Downs was involved with a man, Robert Knickerbocker, who had threatened to end their affair because he did not want children in his life. To this day, Downs has maintained her innocence, and that the story about the highway assailant is true.

Upon conviction Downs was sentenced to life plus fifty years in prison. Initially she was sent to the Oregon Women's Correctional Center. In 1987 she escaped from the OWCC, but was captured ten days later. She was relocated to the Clinton Correctional Facility in

New Jersey—a maximum-security facility. In 2010 she was relocated again to the Valley State Prison for Women in Chowchilla, California. The Valley State Prison has five levels of housing ranging from Level 1, which much like Litchfield has open dormitories to Level 5, which is a SHU (Secured Housing Unit). Downs's story was told in the 1989 made for television movie, *Small Sacrifices*.

Zsa Zsa Gabor

Zsa Zsa Gabor (1932–1997) should probably not be on this list, as her story is more reminiscent of the tabloid fodder discussed above, but it's too funny to leave off. What's noteworthy about Gabor's case is that she was mostly known for being a socialite (she was also an occasional actress and frequent guest on the Merv Griffin Show). She landed three days in county jail for slapping a police officer during a routine traffic stop. For someone known for grace and dignity, she was not so dignified on this occasion.

Gabor for a time was married to Conrad Hilton, who is best known for being Paris Hilton's grandfather (he may also be known for owning a hotel or two). Perhaps there is some causal connection there . . .

Patricia Hearst

The case of Patty Hearst (born 1954), the granddaughter of newspaper magnate William Randolph Hearst (upon whom the Orson Welles movie *Citizen Kane* is loosely based) is truly bizarre.

In 1974 Hearst was at home with her fiancé when members of a dangerous and murderous terrorist group known as the Symbionese Liberation Army

(SLA) broke into her home and kidnapped her at gunpoint. They held her captive for nearly two years. During this time, Hearst claims to have been brainwashed into joining their cause. She assisted them in robbing banks, wielding a machine gun in the crimes. She was also reported to help build small improvised explosive devices. Eventually, she was released by the SLA. It is still not clear whether Hearst had been brainwashed, developed Stockholm Syndrome, or was actually sympathetic to the cause of the SLA.

After her release she was arrested and convicted of robbing banks and the use of a firearm in the commission of a felony. She was initially sentenced to thirty-five years in prison, but that sentence was almost immediately reduced to seven years. She spent two years in solitary confinement (or, as they call it at Litchfield, "the SHU") for security purposes. After twenty-two months President Carter commuted her sentence, releasing her for "time-served." She was eventually pardoned by President Clinton. In recent years she has become quite successful showing dogs in the Westminster Dog show.

Billie Holiday

Billie Holiday (1915–1959), born Eleanora Fagan, was one of the world's great jazz singers. In 1947 Holiday was arrested and, in an extremely public trial (it was billed by the media as "The United States vs. Billie Holiday) where she was quite demonized, convicted of narcotics possession. She was sentenced to one year and one day in Alderson Federal Prison Camp in Alderson, West Virginia, which was The United States' first Federal prison for women—a precursor to modern women's prisons, such as Litchfield.

Like Litchfield, Alderson is not a maximum-security prison; rather, it's a place where the inmates work, have recreational activities, learn crafts, and where great emphasis is placed on vocational training. Initially, the women were housed in small bungalows, and even today there is no barbed-wire anywhere on the premises. Nowadays, the women are housed in large dormitories. Inmates and the media refer to Alderson as "Camp Cupcake," and "Yale" (a pun on "jail").

Karla Homolka

Karla Homolka (born 1970) along with her husband, Paul Bernardo, went on a crime spree in 1991 and 1992 in which they raped and murdered three girls in Ontario, Canada. They video-taped their activities. One of the three victims was Homolka's younger sister, Tammy Homolka. As with Diane Downs, it was initially believed that Homolka participated to appease her husband, who had threatened to leave her. Homolka claimed that her husband forced her to participate in the crimes. The prosecution appeared to buy this to some extent. She was offered a plea bargain, and was convicted of manslaughter, and given a much lighter sentence than Bernardo received (twelve years as opposed to life in prison). After sentencing, the videotape evidence emerged, which showed that Homolka was more involved in the crimes than the prosecution initially believed.

From 1983 to 1987 Homolka was incarcerated in the Prison for Women in Kingston, Ontario. Prison for Women was a maximum-security prison, which was closed in 2000 for a variety of ethical concerns (most notably was the use of LSD in experiments on women). In 1987, Homolka was transferred to Joliet Institution in Quebec. Joliet was a "club fed" style minimum-security prison, where inmates have much freedom to move about the facility, and enjoy many amenities. Just before her release from prison in 2005, Homolke was transferred to Ste-Anne-des-Plaines prison (near Montreal), as officials feared for her life, due to public outrage over her impending release.

Joan of Arc

Joan of Arc (1412–1431) was a French peasant girl who led a group of French soldiers in a number of assaults on the English during the Hundred Years War. Her battles were pivotal in the French turning around the war effort. Joan was eventually captured by the English and charged with over seventy offenses, including witchcraft, heresy, and cross-dressing. In 1431 she was sentenced to death and burned at the stake. Later the Catholic Church made her a saint.

Upon her capture, Joan was held in Beaurevoir Castle, a medieval castle, which held prisoners in tall window-less towers. Her circumstances were not unlike those of the Countess Elizabeth Báthory de Ecsed. Joan attempted to escape by jumping from the tower into a moat seventy feet below. From there she was moved to various facilities until her execution in Rouen, France.

Julia the Elder

Julia the Elder (39 B.C.E.–14 A.D.) was the daughter of Augustus, the first emperor of the Roman Empire. She was also the wife of Tiberius and the grandmother of Caligula. (There may have more than the usual amount of criminal activity in their family). In 2 B.C.E. Augustus charged Julia with adultery and treason. Augustus was motivated largely by a political campaign to promote moral purity. She was found guilty, and sentenced to exile on the island of Pandateria. While it was not a prison, she lived there under very harsh conditions. After five years she was allowed to return to Rome.

Genene Jones

Genene Jones (born 1950) is a former pediatric nurse from Texas, who is believed to have killed somewhere between eleven and forty-six infant children. Allegedly her plan was to inject them with nearly lethal doses of poison, in hopes of reviving them and looking heroic (if so, she was not all that great at determining what constituted a near-lethal dose). Poor hospital record keeping has made the exact number of deaths unclear. She was arrested and convicted in 1985, and was sentenced to ninety-nine years in prison. She is currently being held in Dr. Lane Murry Unit, a women's prison in Texas. Despite her lengthy sentence, she will be released in 2017 due to prison overcrowding.

Amanda Knox

Amanda Knox (born 1987) is an American who, along with her boyfriend, Raffaele Sollecito, was arrested and charged with the stabbing death of her roommate, Meredith Kercher (a British woman), in Italy in 2007. What is particular noteworthy about Knox's case is the on-again-off-again nature of her legal status. In 2009 she was convicted and sentenced to twenty-six years in an Italian prison. In 2011 on appeal she was acquitted and released. She returned to the United States. In her absence, her acquittal was appealed and she was convicted a second time in 2014 (she was given a new trial—Italy has no double jeopardy laws), and in 2015 the Italian Supreme Court overturned her second conviction, finding that the case against her and Sollecito was without foundation and declaring them innocent. From the beginning, leading US forensic experts stated that the forensic evidence was incompatible with Knox and Sollecito's involvement in the murder.

Pussy Riot

In 2012, members of the punk rock collective known as Pussy Riot performed at the Cathedral of Christ the Savior Church in Moscow. The performance had themes that were critical of Russian President Vladimir Putin. Three members of the collective, Nadezhda Tolokonnikova, Maria Alyokhina, and Yekaterina Samutsevich were arrested and charged with hooliganism. Charges against Samutsevich were eventually dropped, but Tolokonnikova and Alyokhina were both convicted and sentenced to two years in a penal colony.

Tolokonnkova was sentenced to IK-14, which is a prison camp, in which inmates are put to hard labor. Alyokhina was sentenced to IK-32, which is for first-time prisoners, and is generally less harsh. Both were treated badly by other prisoners, who generally held Pussy Riot in contempt. They were given early release in late 2013.

Salem Witch Trials

In 1692 and 1693, in Salem and Danvers Massachusetts, thirteen women were hanged on Gallows hill: Bridget Bishop, Rebecca Nurse, Sarah Good, Susannah Martin, Elizabeth Howe, Sarah Wildes, Martha Carrier, Martha Corey, Mary Eastey, Ann Pudeator, Alice Parker, Mary Parker, and Margaret Scott. Their crimes were to have practiced witchcraft by casting spells and by appearing to men in their dreams.

More accused women died in the deplorable prison conditions: Sarah Osborn, Lyndia Dustin, and Ann Foster. Prison cells were small, dark, and filthy. Disease was rampant. No compassion was shown for any reason. Some of the accused were quite elderly and some were young children. The trials were, in part, politically motivated and religious hysteria fueled the fire in the community. If a person was convicted of witchcraft, their land went to the state rather than to their family. By 1697, the trials were considered a tragedy and the victims were officially pardoned.

Martha Stewart

Martha Stewart (born 1941) is a popular television personality, author, publisher and businessperson. She is primarily known for *Martha Stewart Living*, which is an interesting combination of home décor products and media productions (magazines and television programs). Basically, she is famous for being "better than you."

In 2001 Stewart sold some stock when its price fell. She was investigated for securities fraud and insider trading, because it was claimed she sold the stock based on information from her broker. No evidence for these charges could be found, but investigators claimed she had lied to them about a telephone call from her broker, and for that she was convicted in 2004 on charges of conspiracy and obstruction of justice.

She was sentenced to five months in Federal prison and five months' house arrest (with electronic monitoring). She asked to be sent to the Federal Correctional Institution, Danbury, Connecticut (where Piper Kerman served time), but was instead sent to Alderson Federal Prison Camp, the same facility in which Billie

Holiday was incarcerated. Since Holiday's time, Alderson has changed from bungalows to dorms. Like Joliet Institution in Quebec, Alderson is also a "club fed" type institution. Most of the inmates have been charged with either white-collar crimes or recreational drug use.

Stewart became prisoner 55170-054 and was nicknamed "M. Diddy." She later said her prison time had been terrible, and commented: "And everybody tells you, 'Oh, whatever happens to you, it will make you stronger'. Fuck them."

Mary Stuart (Mary, Queen of Scots)

Mary, Queen of Scots, was held for a long period under house arrest. Mary had a habit of not being able to hang onto thrones, though she was heir to many. Mary was the daughter of James V, who was the son of Henry VIII's sister, Margaret Tudor. As a result, she was in the line of succession for two thrones, the throne of Scotland and the throne of England (she was also briefly the Queen of France, by marriage). She was Queen of Scotland from 1542 to 1567, but was forced to abdicate that throne due to scandal and hand it over to her son James (who later became James I of England as well as James VI of Scotland).

Mary was a Catholic and in line for the throne of England. Many Englishman wanted their country to return to Catholicism. As a result, Mary became the center of several political plots to overthrow Elizabeth. Unwilling to kill her cousin, Elizabeth kept her under house arrest for eighteen and a half years. Elizabeth had her guard intercept and decipher her letters. Based on the contents of the letters, Mary was eventually found guilty of plotting the assassination of Elizabeth. Mary was executed on February 7th, 1587, at Fotheringhay Castle.

The executioner missed her neck and instead hit the back of her head with his first stroke. The second stroke severed it. When the executioner tried to hold up her head to show to the spectators, he found himself holding only her wig, the head having fallen to the ground.

The Tower of London's Women Prisoners

The Tower of London—one of the most notorious prisons of all time—also incarcerated some of history's most famous female prisoners. William the Conqueror built the Tower in 1078 and it was used as a prison for 'important' inmates from 1100 to 1952, though parts of it have always been used for other purposes, including sometimes as a royal residence. A massive castle-like structure of several linked buildings, it was built to be imposing—to inspire fear and awe in the population that William had newly conquered. Its location next to the Thames made it quite idyllic. Successions of kings added to it, ultimately expanding the range of places that could hold prisoners.

The Tower has a grisly reputation for the torture that took place behind its walls. In one noteworthy case, a female prisoner was tortured and killed: Anne Askew, a martyr for the Protestant faith. Askew was a gentlewoman and, as was the tradition among gentlewomen at the time, didn't have a choice when it came to the matter of whom she would marry. Her sister was betrothed to a devout Catholic and when that sister dropped dead, Anne was forced to take her place in the betrothal. Askew, a staunch Protestant, didn't much care for the situation in which she found herself. She left her husband and went to London where she was a vocal advocate for her faith. Religion was a touchy subject in England at the time.

Henry VIII's break from Rome pushed the country in a Protestant direction, but he fell short of fully embracing Protestantism. It was dangerous at the time to be an outspoken advocate for any religion. Askew was taken to the Tower and imprisoned there. While in the Tower, she became a political pawn. Courtiers had learned how to push their political agendas—through the King's wives. Henry had painted himself into a corner when it came to religion. He had once been given the title "defender of the faith" by the Pope in part because of the letters he had written in response to the actions of Martin Luther. But now Henry had cut off ties with Rome and declared himself to be "Supreme Head of the Church of England." Despite this break, Henry held firmly to almost all of the doctrines of the Catholic faith. He didn't want to be seen as tolerant of Protestants and his courtiers were aware of that fact. Henry's wife at the time (wife number six, Catherine Parr) was sympathetic to Protestantism. The Anti-Protestant faction at court wanted to out her as a closet Protestant. Their hope was that, with Parr gone, they could find Henry a suitable wife who was not a Protestant and whom they could control. Askew became a tool to achieve that goal.

It was unconventional to torture a woman, but they put Askew on the rack in order to get her to give up the names of other powerful female Protestants. The rack is a rectangular device with a roller at each end. The victim's wrists are attached to one roller and their ankles are attached to the other. The rollers turn, stretching the victim's limbs, causing horrible pain, and, eventually (if the torturer is particularly cruel) detaching the limbs or rendering them permanently ineffective. They encouraged her to name the Queen as a Protestant, but had not reckoned on Askew's willpower.

She refused to name fellow Protestants, and she certainly wouldn't name the Queen. She was eventually sentenced to death by burning. She was so crippled from the torture that she had to be carried in a chair to the pyre. The torture of Askew was infamous. A woman was never again tortured in the Tower (at least not officially). The Tower of London was opened as a tourist location to visitors during the reign of Queen Victoria. At that time, children could purchase a little doll replica of Anne Askew on the rack. Nice of them to think of the kids.

There were several other famous female prisoners in the Tower of London under the reign of Henry VIII. Though their ultimate fates were similar, these prisoners were kept in the Tower under conditions that were much more favorable than Askew's. Noblewomen were not kept in small prison cells. They were kept in fairly comfortable quarters, got to keep their household staff, and were fed well.

One woman who was kept in the Tower in more posh quarters was Anne Boleyn. Anne is commonly held to be one of the most influential royal figures in history. She played a prominent role in the English Reformation. Henry met and fell in love with Anne when she came to court as a lady in waiting to Henry's current wife, Catherine of Aragon. Anne's sister, Mary, had previously been Henry's mistress and Henry hoped that Anne would do the same. She refused. She agreed to sleep with the King only under the condition that he married her. To do this, Henry would obviously have to divorce Catherine. Henry was concerned about the survival of his dynasty, since his marriage to Catherine had not provided him with a male heir. The King attempted to obtain from the Pope an annulment, claiming that his marriage to Catherine was invalid since she had previously been married to his brother, Arthur. The political climate of Europe at the time made it impossible for the Pope to provide the annulment. To marry Anne, the king renounced the Pope, claiming that only kings have a direct line to God.

Henry had hoped that his marriage to Anne would provide him with his desperately desired heir. Anne gave birth to a daughter, the future Elizabeth I, but did not give birth to a live son. Shortly before she was arrested, Anne miscarried what obviously would have been a male child. Henry had grown tired of Anne. She was very outspoken and tried to take an active role in governing the country. Henry did not like that kind of behavior in a woman. He had already found another wife, Anne's lady in waiting, Jane Seymour. He wanted out of the marriage, but there seemed to be no legitimate way out. The king's chancellor, Thomas Cromwell "discovered" evidence that Anne was sleeping with many other men, including her own brother. Anne was charged with adultery and treason. If she were convicted of adultery, she would also be guilty of treason because of the possibility of creating an illegitimate heir to the throne. Anne insisted she was innocent, but she was sentenced to death. As a sign of mercy, Henry honored her request that she be executed by a swordsman from France rather than by an executioner with an ax. She was executed on Friday, May 19th, 1536.

She was not the only one of Henry's wives to suffer this fate. Henry's fifth wife, Catherine Howard, almost thirty years Henry's junior, was also imprisoned and executed in the Tower for the crimes of adultery and treason. Unlike Anne, Catherine was almost certainly guilty of the charges.

The heir that Henry had so desperately longed for was eventually born to his third wife, Jane. Sadly, this son, Edward, didn't live long. Edward VI was crowned at the age of nine and died of tuberculosis just six years later at the age of fifteen. He knew that he would soon die. His father had left instructions for the succession, insisting that if Edward were to die childless, the crown would pass to his daughter Mary Tudor, and were she to die childless, the crown would then pass to his younger daughter, Elizabeth. Edward was Protestant, and spent his short reign making the country into a Protestant kingdom. He knew that his sister Mary would return the country to Catholicism. In a desperate move to keep that from happening, Edward declared that, since his father's marriage to Catherine of Aragon had been illegitimate, Mary was a bastard.

If Mary was a bastard, Elizabeth was as well, since Henry had claimed that his marriage to Anne had also been illegitimate. Edward then made his own plans for the succession—the male heirs of his cousin, Lady Jane Grey (Edward believed that women could not be effective rulers). When he learned that he would die sooner than expected, Edward changed the wording in the succession document to read, "Lady Jane *and* her heirs male." This was a real political coup. Lady Jane was the Queen for nine days. She did not have the support of the people. Mary claimed the throne and threw Jane in the Tower. Jane, just sixteen or seventeen years old, did not want the throne, she had been yet another helpless pawn in a political game. Nonetheless, Mary (who history would know as "Bloody Mary") commanded that her execution take place on 12th of February, 1554.

Not all of the famous prisoners of the Tower of London were put to death. Before becoming Queen, Elizabeth was imprisoned in The Tower under suspicion of playing a role in Wyatt's rebellion, a plot designed to replace Mary with Elizabeth on the throne. She was brought down the Thames and into the Tower through "Traitor's Gate," the same way that her Mother, Anne Boleyn, had been transported to The Tower to live out her final days. Later in life, Elizabeth reported the terror that she felt while in the Tower, knowing that, if she were found guilty, she would certainly be put to death. Ultimately, she was never tried for anything. She was moved from the Tower to Woodstock where she remained under house arrest for another year.

The Tower of London held many of England's most famous prisoners. It's safe to say that it inspired more terror than Litchfield (even a Litchfield with Vee in it!). The Tower continued to occasionally hold prisoners until the 1950s, when the notorious sadistic gangsters, the Kray Twins were confined there. The last prisoner to be killed there, a German spy, was executed in 1941.

Victorian Women in Prison

A number of noteworthy cases of women in prison occurred in England during the reign of Queen Victoria. There were three main types of punishment in Victorian England. The first was imprisonment, which usually also involved hard labor. Hard labor usually entailed working on roads or on the docks. It sometimes involved walking on a treadmill to make flour (though, sometimes, no flour was made—prisoners were made to walk on the treadmill for extended periods of times as punishment). Prison cells were bleak places, usually filthy seven-by-twelve-feet cubes. The next type of punishment was transportation, which meant that the prisoner would be sent away—usually to Australia (though inhabitants of Australia soon grew tired of competing with increasing numbers of criminals for employment). The third form of punishment was death, almost always carried out by hanging the prisoner.

Punishment doled out to Victorian women wasn't exactly what we might, today, think of as proportional to the crime committed. Women were frequently given harsh sentences for very minor crimes. Ancestry.com recently made available online a list of mug shots and parole records for Victorian women. One woman, nineteen-year-old Elizabeth Murphy, was sentenced to five years of hard labor and an additional seven years of police supervision for the grievous offense of stealing an umbrella. Another woman, fifty-nine-year-old, Mary Richards (no relation), was sentenced to five years in prison for stealing 130 oysters. Forty-five-year old Dorcas Mary Snell was sentenced to five years of hard labor for the theft of one slice of bacon.

Other female Victorian criminals were a little more hard-core. Mary Morrison, frustrated that her husband had not paid her weekly allowance. She confronted him at work and threw sulfuric acid in his face, shouting, "Take that—I'll make you worse than you were!" Morrison served three years of a five-year sentence.

There were at least two notorious female serial killers in the Victorian era. The first was Amelia Dyer, known as "the baby farmer" or "The Ogress of Reading." The speculation is that Dyer killed up to four hundred babies and small children. Dyer was a midwife and presented herself to others as a foster parent and adoption facilitator. Times were particularly hard for the poor during this period and many women needed to find someone to care for the child for extended periods of time while they went to work. The children would live with Dyer in exchange for regular payment. At first, Dyer let children die of malnutrition to avoid paying for their care. As time went by, Dyer decided to speed up the process by murdering the children by more pro-active means. She strangled them using white edging tape that she otherwise used for dress -making. She then put the bodies in carpet-bags which she weighed down and dumped in the River Thames. There was one body that she didn't bother to weigh down, and that body was quickly found. The carpet-bag the body was found in contained evidence that led investigators to Dyer. They quickly became suspicious that there might be many more victims. They dragged the river and found six more bodies. Dyer frequently relocated and used many different aliases. As a result, her actual victim count is likely much, much higher. At the trial, Dyer offered an insanity defense, but the jury didn't buy it. They deliberated for just four minutes before delivering a guilty verdict. Dyer spent three weeks in prison before being hanged to death in 1896. Dyer was notorious, and her case inspired a limerick:

> The old baby farmer, the wretched Miss Dyer
> At the Old Bailey her wages is paid.
> In times long ago, we'd 'a' made a big fy-er
> And roasted so nicely that wicked old jade.

A second prolific female serial killer was Mary Ann Cotton. Suspicions were raised when three of her four husbands and eleven of her thirteen children died from "gastric fever." Sure enough, the real cause of death turned out to be arsenic poisoning. Mary was also sentenced to be hanged, but ultimately died of strangulation rather than from a broken neck. Mary, too inspired a rhyme:

> Mary Ann Cotton, she's dead and she's rotten,
> Lying in bed with her eyes wide open.

Sing, sing, oh what should I sing?
Mary Ann Cotton, she's tied up with string.
Where, where? Up in the air.
Selling black puddings, a penny a pair.
Mary Ann Cotton, she's dead and forgotten,
Lying in bed with her bones all rotten.
Sing, sing, what can I sing?
Mary Ann Cotton, tied up with string.

The crimes for which Victorian women were punished were often committed for financial motivations. To get what they wanted, Victorian female criminals would play the cards they were dealt. They would exploit those areas of their lives where they were allowed to have some semblance of power—usually in the domain of marriage and family.

Aileen Wuornos

Aileen Wuornos (1956–2002) was a serial killer operating out of Florida in the 1990s. Wuornous had a troubled childhood. She was the victim of sexual assault more than once. Her mother abandoned her and her father hanged himself in prison. Her maternal grandparents raised her. After her grandmother died, her grandfather kicked her out of the house when she was just fifteen. Aileen started prostituting herself at age eleven, and she survived by engaging in prostitution while she was homeless. Eventually, rather than engaging in sex acts with her customers, she shot them instead. Wuornos killed seven men in 1989 and 1990.

Aileen was incarcerated at the Florida Department of Corrections Broward Correctional Institution. During her incarceration, Wuornos made several accusations against the guards at the facility. She claimed that she was being poisoned, that her food had been urinated on, that her room was bugged, that she was abused, and that her skull was being crushed by "sonic pressure." She was executed at Florida State Prison in October of 2002. Her last meal was a single cup of black coffee.

Andrea Yates

In 2001 Andrea Yates (born 1964), who claimed to be suffering from severe post-partum depression at the time, drowned her five children in a bathtub. In 2002 she pleaded not guilty, but was convicted on five counts of first-degree murder. She was sentenced to life in prison. In 2005 an appeals court overturned her conviction, finding her not guilty by reason of insanity. Prior to her conviction being overturned, Yates was incarcerated at Harris County Jail in Houston, Texas. Since 2005 she has been treated at a minimum-security mental-health treatment facility.

References

Aristotle. 1999. *Nicomachean Ethics*. Hackett.

Barnhill, Anne. 2014. What Is Manipulation? In Coons and Weber 2014.

Beauvoir, Simone de. 1976. *The Ethics of Ambiguity*. Citadel Press.

Bentham, Jeremy 2007 [1789]. *An Introduction to the Principles of Morals and Legislation*. Dover.

———. 2008 [1787]. *Panopticon: Or, the Inspection House*. Dodo.

———. 2009 [1830]. *Rationale of Punishment*. Cornell University Library.

Biography.com website. 2015. Aileen Wuornos. <www.biography.com/people/aileen-wuornos-11735792# early-life>.

Blumberg, Jess. 2007. A Brief History of the Salem Witch Trials. Smithsonian.com. <www.smithsonianmag.com/history/a-brief-history-of-the-salem-witch-trials-175162489/?no-ist>.

Bossip. 2014. Locked Up: 13 Famous Women Who Spent Time in Jail. <http://bossip.com/1077648/locked-up-13-famous-women-who-spent-time-in-jail>.

Bureau of Justice Statistics. 2014. Recidivism of Prisoners Released in 30 States in 2005: Patterns from 2005 to 2010. <www.bjs.gov/index.cfm?ty=pbdetail&iid=4987>.

Carnegie, Dale. 1998 [1936]. *How to Win Friends and Influence People*. Pocket Books.

Cervantes, Miguel de. 2003 [1614]. *Don Quixote*. Penguin.

Criminal Justice Degrees Guide. 2015. 10 Most Infamous Female Criminals.

References

<www.criminaljusticedegreesguide.com/features/10-most-infamous-female-criminals.html>.

Blumenthal-Barby, J.S. 2014. A Framework for Assessing the Moral Status of Manipulation. In Coons and Weber 2014.

Coons, Christian, and Michael Weber. 2014. *Manipulation: Theory and Practice*. Oxford University Press.

Daily Mail Reporter. 2015. Victorian Bad Girls: Police Mugshots of 19th Century Women Criminals Revealed. *Daily Mail* (July 9th). <www.dailymail.co.uk/news/article-1360345/Ancestry-uk-Police-mugshots-19th-century-women-criminals-revealed.html>.

Descartes, René. 2001. *Meditations and Other Metaphysical Writings*. Penguin.

Egginton, William. 2011. 'Quixote', Colbert, and the Reality of Fiction. *New York Times* (September 25th).

Flynn, Bernard. 2011. Maurice Merleau-Ponty. The Stanford Encyclopedia Philosophy.

Foucault Michel. 1977. *Discipline and Punish: The Birth of the Prison*. Pantheon.

Greene, Robert. 2007. *The 33 Strategies of War*. Joost Eiffers.

The Huffington Post. 2014. Orange Is the New Black Opening Credits Feature Real, Formerly Incarcerated Women. <www.huffingtonpost.com/2013/08/20/orange-is-the-new-black-opening-credits_n_3786127.html>.

Hunter, Evan. 1984 *Lizzie*. Arbor House.

Jacobs, Matthew. 2013. Celebrities in Jail: 25 Stars Who've Served Time Behind Bars. <www.huffingtonpost.com/2013/03/20/celebrities-in-jail_n_2917945.html>.

Kant Immanuel. 1996. *The Metaphysics of Morals*. Cambridge University Press.

Kerman, Piper. 2010. *Orange Is the New Black: My Year in a Women's Prison*. Random House.

Kurtz, Paul. 2007. *What Is Secular Humanism?* Prometheus.

Machiavelli, Niccolò. 1998. *The Prince*. University of Chicago Press.

McGinn, Colin. 2014. *MindFucking: A Critique of Mental Manipulation*. Routledge.

Merleau-Ponty, Maurice. 1968. *The Visible and the Invisible*. Northwestern University Press.

———. 2013. *Phenomenology of Perception*. Routledge.

References

National Institute on Drug Abuse. 2008. Relapse Rates for Drug
Addiction Are Similar to Those of Other Well-Characterized
Chronic Illnesses. <www.drugabuse.gov/publications/
addiction-science/relapse/relapse-rates-drug-addiction-are-
similar-to-those-other-well-characterized-chronic-ill>.

Nietzsche, Friedrich. 1978. *A Nietzsche Reader*. Penguin.

———. 2000. *Basic Writings of Nietzsche*. Modern Library.

———. 2012. *Thus Spoke Zarathustra*. Simon and Brown.

Noggle, Robert. 1996. Manipulative Actions: A Conceptual and
Moral Analysis. *American Philosophical Quarterly* 33:1.

Pierce, Kristen. 2013. *True Tales from Women's Jail: Diary of a
Female Prisoner*. Knox Press.

Plato. 1997. *Plato: Complete Works*. Hackett.

Rathbone, Cristina. 2006. *A World Apart: Women, Prison, and Life
Behind Bars*. Random House.

Rawls John. 1999 [1971]. *A Theory of Justice*. Harvard University
Press.

Rothman, Michael. 2014. Martha Stewart Gets Candid about Her
Past Prison Time. ABC News online (October 27th).

Sartre, Jean-Paul. 1988 [1965]. The Humanism of Existentialism.
In *Essays in Existentialism*. Citadel.

———. 1989. *No Exit and Three Other Plays*. Vintage.

———. 1993 [1943]. *Being and Nothingness*, Washington Square
Press.

Stanley, Jason. 2015. *How Propaganda Works*. Princeton University Press.

Weir, Alison. 2007. *The Six Wives of Henry VIII*. Grove Atlantic.

Wittgenstein, Ludwig. 1998. *Last Writings on the Philosophy of
Psychology*. Blackwell.

———. 1999. *Philosophical Investigations*. Blackwell.

Wolf, Susan. 2010. *Meaning in Life and Why It Matters*. Princeton
University Press.

Wolters, Cleary. 2015. *Out of Orange: A Memoir*. Harper.

Perpetrators' Rap Sheets

CHELSI BARNARD "QUEEN BITCH" ARCHIBALD has an MA in English from Weber State University. She writes television recaps for Socialite Life, a prominent celebrity gossip blog. She enjoys long hot showers, gourmet meals sans tampon, and a king sized bed with high-count cotton sheets. She would not fare well at Litchfield Penitentiary. But if necessary, she could craft a decent shank.

ROD "HOT ROD" CARVETH is Director of Graduate Studies for the School of Global Journalism and Communication at Morgan State University. He is co-editor of *Justified and Philosophy* and a contributor to *Boardwalk Empire and Philosophy* and *The Good Wife and Philosophy*. His experience with the penal system has been limited to an evening in a prison cell for being too exuberant after consuming one-too-many adult beverages.

MYISHA "NATTY DREAD" CHERRY is a philosopher and essayist. She's interested in moral psychology and finds every inmate at Litchfield prison an intriguing philosophical case study. A former educator at the *Fortune Society* and former Faculty Associate at the John Jay College *Institute for Criminal Justice Ethics*, she is currently pursuing a PhD in philosophy at the University of Illinois, Chicago. Myisha is also a blogger at the Huffington Post and has taught philosophy at the college level for over ten years. One of her greatest lessons in life is never to trust anyone with a porn stach. A self-described "cool geek," a perfect afternoon for her would be to talk philosophy (in accents) with Taystee and Poussey in the library.

CHRISTINA A. "THE TONGUE" DiEDOARDO is a criminal defense lawyer who earned her JD at the William S. Boyd School of Law in Las Vegas, Nevada. Since then, she's tried to even out the odds for the Sophia Bursets of the world while not shanking the Piper Chapmans of the courtroom or telling judges "It's a metaphor, you potato with eyes!" a la Pennsatucky. Alas, she does not always succeed in reaching the latter two goals.

LEIGH "THE ILLUSION" DUFFY lectures in philosophy at SUNY Buffalo State College. She teaches courses such as Philosophy of Mind, Philosophy of Emotion, Philosophy of Yoga, and Meaning of Life. She's also a certified yoga instructor (but her favorite *Orange Is the New Black* character isn't Yoga Jones—it's Taystee). Leigh has never been to prison, but she is the mother of two small children so she is fairly certain she can relate to the women of Litchfield in that her things are always being stolen, she's unable to use the bathroom in private, and she's been on the receiving end of a thrown pie.

CHARLENE "RACK 'EM UP" ELSBY is an Assistant Professor at Indiana University-Purdue University, Fort Wayne. Having completed her PhD on Aristotle, she naturally assumed that *Orange Is the New Black* would be an enlightening program about the ontology of perceptibles. (It isn't, for the record.)

STEPHEN "RADIO FACE" FELDER is an intellectual and cultural historian. He is currently Professor of Humanities at Irvine Valley College, a campus that has recently become smoke-free. This has forced him to step up his training program for cigarette-courier roaches—a move that has made him very popular with his more desperate colleagues. He holds a PhD in history from the University of California, Irvine.

RICHARD "GANGRENE" GREENE is a Professor of Philosophy at Weber State University. He's also serves as Executive Chair of the Intercollegiate Ethics Bowl. He's co-edited a number of books on pop culture and philosophy including *Girls and Philosophy*, *Dexter and Philosophy*, *Quentin Tarantino and Philosophy*, *Boardwalk Empire and Philosophy*, and *The Sopranos and Philosophy*. Richard worries that someday when he is older he too may have them TV titties.

RACHEL "PRUNO PRO" ROBISON-GREENE is a PhD Candidate in Philosophy at UMass Amherst. She is co-editor of *The Golden Compass and Philosophy*, *Dexter and Philosophy*, *Boardwalk Empire and Philosophy*, and *Girls and Philosophy*. She has contributed chapters to *Quentin Tarantino and Philosophy*, *The Legend of Zelda and Philosophy*, *Zombies, Vampires, and Philosophy*, and *The Walking Dead and Philosophy*. Rachel is so inspired by *Orange Is the New Black* that she wears maxipads on her feet while showering at home.

CHRISTOPHER "BUSTA KILLER" HOYT teaches philosophy at Western Carolina University, and has managed to stay out of jail for more than ten years. Writing for academic journals makes him grumpier than Healy, so writing about one of his favorite television shows was like a furlough from his day job. He's always happy to have a long conversation about television or movies in his down time, but if you want to join him, please bring the sparkling wine and leave the malt liquor to Piper.

CHRISTOPHER "THE BAPTIST" KETCHAM holds a doctorate in Curriculum and Instruction from the University of Texas at Austin. His research and writing interests are ethics, risk management, and social justice from his modest Panopticon in Pennsylvania. Just think of it . . . What if Jeremy Bentham were a member of Congress? Perish the thought!

ROB "LUCKY" LUZECKY is a lecturer at Indiana University—Purdue University Fort Wayne. When he's not teaching students how to stay out of Litchfield, he spends his time contemplating aesthetics, metaphysics, the ontology of social objects, and the writings of Roman Ingarden. His lifelong goal is to figure out how to get free cans of coffee from the commissary.

COURTNEY "KNOW-IT-ALL" NEAL is an educator and graduate of DePaul University; her interests are in narrative study and why we tell stories. Especially other people's stories. It's important not to be the moon.

JEFF "CLOCKER" STEPHENSON holds a PhD in Philosophy and is a part-time lecturer at Montana State University and Montana Tech. He may or may not have broken the law dozens of times, but he doesn't want to address the issue because he knows the State now surveils everything, including the content of this book.

SETH M. "HOUSE HOOCH" WALKER teaches courses in religious studies, philosophy, and humanities at the University of Central Florida. He's also one of the founding editors of *Nomos Journal*—an online magazine engaging the intersection between religion and popular culture. Seth has contributed chapters to *Jurassic Park and Philosophy* and *The Ultimate Walking Dead and Philosophy*. He spends his waking hours trying to make something as meaningful and beautiful as he can out of life . . . and, like Piper, cringes at the sight of a grimy muck sink.

SARA "THE BALLER" WALLER received her PhD from Loyola University Chicago and is currently an Associate Professor of Philosophy at Montana State University. She studies the minds of co-operative predators, ranging from humans to dolphins to wolves and coyotes, and seeks to decode the vocalizations essential to social actions—like conspiring to keep power and orchestrating the incarceration of those who threaten that power.

Index